Elijah Russell Morse

A Collection of Original Poems

Elijah Russell Morse

A Collection of Original Poems

ISBN/EAN: 9783744705172

Printed in Europe, USA, Canada, Australia, Japan

Cover: Foto ©Thomas Meinert / pixelio.de

More available books at **www.hansebooks.com**

A COLLECTION

OF

ORIGINAL POEMS

BY
ELIJAH RUSSELL MORSE.

Dedication.

THIS LITTLE BOOK

I DEDICATE

TO

MY CHILDREN.

Contents.

God Everywhere,	9
Can We Forget Our Patriot Dead?,	10
Return of May,	12
Man is Full of Frailty,	13
Slavery,	14
My Native Land,	15
O, My Country,	16
Return of Spring,	17
The Boys in Blue,	19
Genius,	20
Can We Forget?,	21
Green Mountain State,	22
Sweet Summer, Thou Art Gone,	23
Autumn,	24
My Childhood's Home,	25
Niagara,	27
Winter, 1843-44,	28
Haste, Thou Sinner,	29
Hope,	30
Acrostic—Minnie Evelyn Morse,	31
The Prayer for Life,	32
Hymn from the 96th Psalm,	34
Life is Short,	35
The Tolling Bell,	36
Song for Winter,	37
The Name of Morse,	38
Funeral Hymn,	39
From Earth I Soared Away,	40
The Bobolink,	42
Scraps,	43
Zack and I,	44
Snow,	45
Mourn,	46
Reliance on Heaven,	47
Flowers,	48
Gems,	49
Almost Eight,	49
Doubt and Fear,	50
Return of May, 1844,	52
Repeal,	53
The New Year,	54
November,	55
Joy and Sadness,	56
My Father and Mother,	57
Could We But Know,	58
Memorial Hymn.—Bedeck Their Graves,	59
Death,	60
Waiting for the Rain,	61
A Hymn of Praise and Invocation,	62
Illinois,	63
Stern Winter Reigns,	64
Strains Divine,	64
May,	65
Speak Kindly,	68
Tears,	69
The Poor,	71
All Nature Sings,	73
A Sister's Dying Farewell,	74
Acrostic.—Orpha Shipman,	75
Spring,	76
Is There a Day Without a Morn,	77
There's Beauty but it Fades Away,	78
Spring Appears,	80
Grant,	81
Campaign Song,	84
Acrostic.—Susan C. Lowell,	85
Meter,	86
June Training Day,	87
Childhood,	88
For Adam's Race,	90
Yes, in Retirement and Alone,	91
Acrostic.—Betsy Jane Lowell,	92
My Mountain Home Song,	93
Where Shall the Poet Find a Theme?,	94
Our Life a Dream,	95
Extracts,	96
The Cold, Chill Hand of Death,	97
Ogle County in Rhyme,	98
The Maiden's Choice,	100
It is a Shame,	102
The Heavens Thy Power Proclaim,	103
Come, Blooming Health,	104

The Dying Christian,	106
A Vermont Snow Storm,	108
Youth,	109
To the Moon,	110
Acrostic.—Orra Laporte,	112
The Parting Hour,	113
Take the Bible as Your Guide,	114
Memorial Hymn.—O, Lightly, Softly Tread,	115
On the Death of Torrey,	116
A Light is on the Mountains,	118
Calvary,	120
Mount Pulaski,	121
They Will not Let Them Go,	122
A Brighter Day is Dawning,	123
Old Winter is Here,	125
O, Thou Almighty King,	126
Gems,	127
Hope,	127
Pity,	128
We All are Frail,	130
My Soul is Longing for its Rest,	132
Columbia,	133
The Past,	135
The Land of Rest,	136
Centennial Hymn,	137
The Present,	140
The Dead,	141
Time Rolls On,	142
Ten O'clock is Saying,	143
Pay the Printer,	144
Acrostic.—Laura Ann Thomas,	145
Thanksgiving Day,	146
'Tis Noon,	149
The Sea of Life,	150
Reverie,	151
Welcome to Jennie Lind,	152
The Future,	153
Acrostic.—Sarah C. Havena,	154
Campaign Song,	155
Life is a Struggle,	156
After the Storm,	156
Acrostic.—Ann M. Littlefield,	157
The Silent Land,	158
Acrostic.—Jerusha Hill Thomas,	159
Summer,	160
The Ashtabula Horror,	161
The Melancholy Smile,	162
Winter,	163
The Cuckoo,	164
The Maiden's Prayer,	166
Acrostic.—Mary Jane Thomas,	167
Welcome to Summer,	168
Go West,	170
How Happy is the Heavenly Throng,	171
Then When Coldness Clogs This Clay,	172
Turn Now to God,	173
Acrostic.—William Cullen Warner,	174
The Burial Ground,	175
A Hymn of Praise,	178
Spring Again,	180
Acrostic.—Oscar E. Morse,	180
May Day,	181
Melancholy Thoughts,	182
Sabbath Morn,	183
Can We Forget the Men of Old,	184
The Joys of Earth,	185
Acrostic.—Beauty,	186
O, Let Me Rest,	187

Salutatory.

When first to myself, by one of our family, it was proposed to have my Poems published in pamphlet or book form, I was very much pleased with the idea, as I had been thinking for years, who or what person, or by what agency my productions in verse would be looked up and brought together, looked up and brought to light, so scattered and dilapidated, many of them forty and fifty years of age, and from that to the present time.

Quite a good many of the older ones have been published, and more or less of them have been lost; and some I have recalled by most pertinacious thinking, and thus have brought them back to memory, from oblivion, by a word or a line, and thus giving an index to the piece or title.

While looking up, revising, and copying the old, I have composed and added quite a number of new ones, which I hope and trust, will be appreciated by my children as a legacy of some worth, at least, from one of Three Score Years and Ten.

And may a perusal of these productions of my thoughts and pen inspire my children, and children's children,—inspire them with love of Country, Freedom, Father, Mother, and of Nature's God.

Elijah Russell Morse.

God Everywhere.

Where dwelleth God? O, everywhere,
   Among the creatures of His care.
In every place, in every spot.
   We cannot go where He is not.

In every beam that morning throws;
   In every star that brightly glows;
In every drop of glittering dew;
   In every rainbow's blended hue.

In every fair and fragile flower,
   We see displayed His sovereign power.
O, everywhere His works are seen;
   In the grass that springs, so bright and green.

In every leaf, in every blade,
   In every thing which God hath made,
In sparkling rills, in ocean's foam;
   And in the sky's resplendent dome.

In light-winged clouds, of angel form;
   And in the lightning, in the storm.
In high and low, in great and small;
   In man the noblest of them all!

His radiance fills, enthroned on high,
   Our earth, and worlds beyond the sky.
Nor thought can soar, nor tongue can tell,
   Where God in spirit doth not dwell!

Can We Forget Our Patriot Dead?

Can we forget our patriot dead,
    Who for their home and country died;
Our fallen ones, who for us bled,—
    The battle-scarred,—who Death defied?

Can we forget the April morn,
    When Sumpter, pierced, and bleeding fell,
Our flag struck down, and soiled, and torn,
    By rebel hands,—with shot and shell?

Can we forget the wild alarm,—
    When tidings like the lightning flew
Along the wires,— The call to arm,—
    And wildest notes the trumpets blew?

Can we forget the parting tear;
    The father, mother, brother, son?
Can we forget to freedom dear,
    Their crown of glory won?

Can we forget our Lincoln's fall?
    Our greatest, noblest martyr slain:
The darkest crime, foulest of all,
    That can a Nation's records stain?

Shall we forget to come each year,
    With reverent hearts, our tribute bring,
And shed for them the pensive tear,
    And strew the sweetest flowers of Spring.

Above their honored, sacred dust,—
   While thoughts will wander far away,—
To God we yield the sacred trust,—
   Of guarding well their moldering clay,

Of those who sleep in unknown graves,—
   Who fell in battle's fiercest strife:
O'er them blest Freedom's banner waves,—
   Who died to save the Nation's life.

As long as sacred love can burn,
   Within an aching human breast,
So shall our hearts towards them yearn,
   Our martyred heroes now at rest.!

Return of May.

We welcome thee, returning May,
    Thou lovely daughter of the Spring;
We welcome thee this holiday,
    For thou dost joy and gladness bring.

Blest health is on thy blooming cheek,
    And youth and beauty in thine eyes;
Ah! lovely maiden, mild and meek,
    Thou art a child of Paradise.

And thou hast come, our earth to bless
    With fairy breeze, refreshing showers;
With all thy beauties numberless,
    To beautify this earth of ours.

Sweet music breathes on every gale,
    Creation's chorus joins the lay;
All welcome thee, and gladly hail
    Again thy smiles, returning May.

Man is Full of Frailty.

Man is full of frailty,
  God is full of power;
His kingdom lasts forever,
  Man's only for an hour.

Man stands pale and trembling,
  When man he only sees;
But God, when storms o'erwhelming
  Rage, commands and all is peace.

Man glories for a while,
  But soon his joy is fled;
Then sorrow shades a smile,
  And sinks him 'mong the dead.

O, then while frail is man,
  His glory but an hour;
Life measured by a span;
  And strengthless is his power.

In God let us confide,
  Whose glory, strength and power,
While on life's stormy tide,
  To us will be a tower,—

A tower whose bulwarks are of old,
  Whose walls are built on high;
A strong defense, a mighty hold,
  Encircling earth and sky.

In Him we sure will trust,
   His arm is strong to save;
And though we moulder back to dust,
   He'll rescue from the grave.

Slavery.

Woe, the land whose soil is cursed
   With Slavery's unrelenting hand;
Tho' seem it prosperous at first,
   Woe is reserved for such a land!

Though sweat and toil, and blood and tears,
   The harden'd Lord may yet devour;
He cannot stay the storm of years,
   Gathering to crush Oppression's power.

Woe, woe, to those who lend their aid,
   And help to bind the galling chain;
They write their name with human blood,—
   Themselves and country wear the stain.

Lo! Generations, yet unborn,
   Shall curse them for their sinful deed;
Shall heap on them a world of scorn,
   When Freedom shall no longer bleed.

My Native Land.

Again among the hills I stand,
Hills of my own dear native land,
   Where mountain peaks in grandeur rise.
I tread once more, where childhood, sweet,
Prattled and played with wandering feet,—
   Ye greet again my longing eyes.!

O, youth and age, how soon they pass,—
'Tis like the mist, or withering grass;—
   They come and go, they pass away;
Or like the verdant hills that bloom,
They blossom, flourish, find a tomb,
   And mingle with their mother clay.

'Tis sad, yet sweet,—unbidden tears,
Will start, to think of other years,
   Of joys, and sorrows,—lot of all.
I hear the brooklet's merry flow,
The cricket's chirp of long ago,
   And voices from the woodlands call!

Adieu,—the autumn's glittering sheen
Has donned its robe of changing green;
   Reflected in the lake below:
Whose placid waters on its breast,
Lie quiet as a babe at rest,
   Or, river's still, majestic flow.

Old age will come, and stern decay;
But O, thy hills pass not away.
　　The mountains too, O! they shall stand,
Like truth eternal they shall be.
Sadly I turn away from thee,—
　　Farewell, my own dear native land.

In my old home, Sept. 22, 1876.

O, My Country.

O, my country, 'tis oft I think of Thee;
And thinking, wish that Thou wert truly free.
Wish Thou wert free from Slavery's galling chain,
So that Thy glory be not found in vain.

My country, wake! Shake off the gloom of years;
Set millions free, and stay their bitter tears.
Let human rights now move thy inmost soul,
And love of man thy actions all control.

Shake off the sin which binds a curse on Thee;
My country wake, and be Thou truly free.
Heaven cries aloud, put off a Nation's shame,
Let Freedom live, as well as have a name.

Return of Spring.

I am with you, I am with you,
　　Though for me you've waited long;
Now most joyfully I greet you,
　　With my bright and happy throng.
For I've broke the icy fetters
　　Of old Winter's dreary reign,
And the snow-wreaths I have wasted
　　From the valley, hill and plain.

I have wandered o'er the mountains,
　　And the merry rills are free;
And again the sparkling fountains
　　In the sunlight welcome me.
Lo, all nature is awaking
　　From her long and dreary sleep,
As she bids me to be joyful,
　　And no more in silence weep.

Loud her anthem now is swelling,
　　And it fills the balmy air;
On the wings of love 'tis wafted,
　　While she kneels to God in prayer.
And she smiles to meet her loved ones,
　　Whom she counted but as slain;
And her great heart's nobly beating
　　At the sound of my dear name.

I have breathed upon the forests,
    As I did in days of yore;
I have come with gentle showers,
    And old earth is young once more.
And the grass is greenly springing,
    And the flowers awake from death,
As with gentle hand I touch them,
    Kiss them with my balmy breath.

Wake then Mortal, wake from sadness,
    Let thy heart with nature bloom;
Swell the song of joy and gladness,
    Hope for me beyond the tomb.
When life's struggle all is over,
    And its wintry storms are past,
O, then meet me, joyous greet me,
    Where I shall forever last.

The Boys in Blue.

Brave boys in blue, to freedom true,
    Your cause is just and holy;
Go marching on, brave boys in blue,
    Till the final victory.

CHORUS.

Three cheers, ho! for the boys in blue, O!
Three cheers for the soldier boys in blue!

When Sumpter spoke, 'mid flame and smoke,
    And cannon's awful thunder;
It shook the land, on every hand,
    With horror and with wonder.

CHORUS.

It told the North, the trait'rous South
    Had sounded war's loud rattle,
In wild alarm it bade it arm,
    And fight the mighty battle.

CHORUS.

Then our boys in blue, indignant flew
    From mountain, hill and valley;
From prairies, wide to ocean's tide,
    Around the flag to rally.

CHORUS.

The good old flag, the Union flag,
　By traitor hands made gory;
They seized it then, those patriot men,
　And bore it on to glory.

CHORUS.

Till Treason's breath, is lost in death,
　Go, bear the starry banner.
Till land, and sea, shall peaceful be,
　And swell the loud Hosanna.

Genius.

Genius kindles its own fires,
With poetry the soul inspires,
It feeds upon its own bright flame,
And records high its deeds of fame.

Say'st thou that Genius e'er shall die?
That spark of Immortality!
Nay, nothing here so strong can bind
The Genius of Immortal mind.

Can We Forget?

Oh, can we, shall we e'er forget,
   Sumpter's and Lincoln's fall;
Those April morns, in sorrow set,—
   The wormwood and the gall?

The darkness, dread, and gloom that came
   In that eventful hour;
The servile slave, who clanked the chain,—
   The master's league of power?

The threat, the blow—our flag struck down,
   And trampled in the dust;
When spake a voice, Jehovah's own,—
   " Freemen, arise, ye must."

Can we forget the parting tear,
   The father, brother, son?
Can we forget to Freedom dear
   Their crown of glory won?

Long as a sacred fire shall burn
   Within a human breast,
So shall our hearts toward them yearn,—
   Our heroes now at rest.

O, yes, as long as stars shall shine,
   And sun shall rise and set;
As long as Freedom hath a shrine,
   We cannot them forget.

O'er them the dear old flag shall wave,
　The flag 'neath which they fell;
And Freedom's sons o'er their graves,
　Shall dirge and anthem swell.'

Green Mountain State.

Green Mountain State, thy stalwart men
Have honored thee with sword and pen;
Thy daughters, fair, are brave and true,
As ever smiled 'neath heaven's blue.
Here is no lord, or servile slave,
No room to live, or find a grave.
Time's changes come, and bring decay,
But O, thy hills pass not away;
Thy mountains green, majestic stand,
Like truth, eternal they shall be.
O, in our constellation, bright,
Thou art a star of glorious light;
A little giant, proud and grand;
Helping to guard a Nation's fate,
With power and justice of a state.
Thy name, and fame shall live for aye,
Shall swell the anthem of the free;
In all the ages yet to be,
Throughout our own, and every land.

Sweet Summer, Thou Art Gone.

Sweet Summer, thou art gone,
   And Autumn now is here;
We meet thee with a smile,
   A kiss, and with a tear.

We meet thee with a smile,
   For thy beauteous dawn of light;
We meet thee with a kiss,
   For blushing sweetly into night.

We meet thee with a tear,
   We knew most passing well,
That thou wouldst go and leave us,
   And bid us all farewell.

Yet Summer, lovely Summer,
   Shall we not meet again,
When snow-wreaths have wasted,
   From valley, hill and plain?

When Spring-buds of promise
   Have blossomed into flowers,
And-song birds have cheered us,
   'Mid sunshine and 'mid showers.

Again with loving hearts,
   O, dearest may we meet,
And tread among thy roses,
   With strong and stainless feet.

Autumn.

Autumn, I love thee—"Season of mellow
Fruitfulness, of the sere and yellow leaf."
What hand of art, most perfect, so nicely paint
As Nature doth for Thee? with colors bright,
Arrayed, blending, are those of richest hue.
What gorgeous splendor in the scene around.
In thy noon-tide glory, how beautiful,
How grand, and how sublime.
      The forest old,
Stands decked in thy rich vesture, resplendent,
Stately and tall, with age honorable;
From years of youthful bloom, to manhood's prime,
Budding and blossoming, in time olden,
And meeting the chilling blasts of winter,
As the seasons rolled their eternal rounds.
There's such an awe in thy solemn grandeur,
It makes me love thee more,—more than all else;
'Tis this which leads my soul to contemplate
The wondrous works of God, Some loved retreat,
It seeks, wrapped in its clayey tenement.
To commune with Him, maker of all things,
Who puts thy glory on.
      Alas! how soon
The never-staying hand of time, will rob
Thee of thy golden locks, and fling around
The pall of gloom, thyself in Winter's arms.

My Childhood's Home.

Green is the turf whereon I trod,
   In childhood's merry glee;
Where first I learned the name of God,
   Upon my mother's knee.

CHORUS.

My childhood's home, my childhood's home,
   I now no longer see;
Yet, when afar I from it roam,
   'Tis mine in memory.

The merry brook went prattling by;
   Its banks were bright and green;
Singing to me its lullaby,—
   But now, how changed the scene.

'Twas there our humble cottage stood,
   With sunny bank before,
From whence came forth the prattling brood,—
   Aye then,—but now no more.

There flowed the sweetly murmuring rill,
   In accents soft and low;
Though years have flown, 'tis whispering still
   Of scenes, long, long ago.

CHORUS.

My childhood's home, my childhood's home,
   I now no longer see;
Yet, when afar I from it roam,
   'Tis mine in memory.

Father and mother, there were mine;
   Brothers and sisters dear;
And there the altar's sacred shrine,—
   But now, no longer there.

And there were those who roamed with me
   The wildwood and the dell;
Whose hearts were young, and gay, and free;
   We meet no more.—Farewell.

Stern Death has found his victims there,
   Has laid them in the tomb;
In morning's life, the young and fair,
   Cut off in youthful bloom.

Age, youth, and friends, and time have fled,
   'Mid changes, great and small,
But O, ye living, and ye dead,
   I love, I love ye all.

CHORUS.

My childhood's home, my childhood's home,
   I now no longer see;
Yet when afar I from it roam,
   'Tis mine in memory.

Niagara.

I come and homage pay to thee, —
So terrible, haughty and free: —
O, wonderful Niagara.

I stand upon thy rugged shore; —
I hear thy plunging waters pour; —
I *see*, I *feel*, thy mighty power.

Oh! cataract of olden time; —
Most wonderful of any clime; —
Oh! who can *paint* the scenes sublime?

Thy awful grandeur fills the soul, —
With wonder, — far beyond control, —
Supremely felt, — and yet untold.

Oh, who can picture long ago;
When first thou met Ontario; —
Or broad Atlantic far below?

Oh, whence, or where thy waters sped;
When first upon thy rocky bed,
The light of day its glory shed?

Far o'er the vista of long years, —
Is thrown the veil of misty tears, —
Eternity thy echo hears.

Superior, and Huron, come,
And Michigan, and Erie, dumb, —
And find in thee a living tomb.

Speed on, majestic, proud and free,—
A world pays homage unto thee,—
Oh, wonderful Niagara.

At Niagara, Sept. 28, 1876.

Winter, 1843=44.

Stern Winter reigns o'er all the land,
   With undiminished sway;
He graspeth all with icy hand,
   Who cometh in his way.

The snow-clad hills, and mountains bold,
   Lift up their hoary head,
And seem like one who hath grown old,
   Their youth and beauty fled.

The crystal Frost bedecks the trees,
   Or deathly broods the flower;
Ah, yes, the cold and chilly breeze,
   Bespeaks old Winter's power.

With icy fetters binds the streams,
   The sparkling, flowing rill,
Where silent, lay the cold sunbeams,
   And all is lone and still.

And saddened Nature sleepeth on,
   Deep buried in her tomb;
And heedeth not, with hope forlorn,
   Amid the deep'ning gloom.

Haste Thou Sinner.

Haste thou sinner, lone and weary,
   For danger lieth in the road;
And the way is dark and dreary,
   While a wanderer from thy God!

Speed thee on thy darksome journey,
   For howling tempests gather 'round;
And soon the bolts of heaven's thunder,
   May break and pour its awful sound.

Then poor sinner, where for shelter,
   Where wilt thou flee to hide thy head;
In thy blood then wilt thou welter,
   Oh, shun the wrath of God most dread.

Oh, methinks I hear you saying,
   I now will turn to God and live;
While the bolts of wrath he's staying,
   My soul, my all to Him I'll give.

So, that when His fury, bursting,
   Upon a world of sin and woe;
While His arrows, barb'd are piercing,
   Quite the guilty sinner through.

I may find a place in heaven,
   A happy home where angels dwell;
And there with all that are forgiven,
   The song of ransomed spirits swell.

Hope.

Hope, 'tis a word both great and good,
    Most mighty in its sway;
For many years strong hath it stood,
    While chasing doubt away.

A tower and bulwark of defense,
    To all who in it trust;
A light, a joy to feeble sense,
    A guide for sinful dust.

Hope,' tis a gem—itself the thing
    Which bids us look and see;
Which soars on Faith's sublimest wings,
    Into futurity.

Hope, like an anchor to the soul,
    Guides safely o'er the deep,
Where giant waves, and billows roll,—
    Her vigil there doth keep.

Our bark, of winds and waves the sport,
    Glides joyfully along;
With Hope to guide us, and escort,
    With her bright banner flung.

By Hope, through Faith, the Christian looks,
    For Grace, and Strength divine;
And with the key of Faith unlocks,
    And views a fairer clime.

He hopes that when his days are past,
And all his work is done;
To sing a song of joy at last,
Which was on earth begun!

February, 1842

Acrostic.

MINNIE EVELYN MORSE.

Many are the joys and sorrows,
In this life, 'tis ours to know.
Never comes to us to-morrows,—
Never, while we onward go.
In to-day,—of golden moments;
Ever find we weal or woe. ?

Envy not the lot of others;
Virtue is a priceless boon.
Endear thyself to sisters, brothers,
Let sunlight in thy heart find room.
Youth and beauty never die,—
No,—eternal are the ages. ?

Morning scatters night away.
O, let us as we turn life's pages,
Resolve, to better live each day.
So may we seek,—contentment find;
Ever in heart, ever in mind. ?

The Prayer for Life.

A Nation's prayers ascend to-day,
From loyal hearts incessantly;
To God, the President may live,
That He to him, yet strength will give,
So he may rise from bed of pain,
To bless us and the world again.

Oh! why should murderous hand be raised,
To take his life, to end his days?
Oh! God, it is Thy mystery,
We vainly search, we cannot see,
Why he who first among us stood,
Why he so strong, noble and good,
Friend of his race, of sin the foe,
Should sink beneath a maniac's blow.

The Nation's pulses throb and thrill,
With his so quick, so strong of will;
Through all the day with fever heat,
In unison together beat;
Through all the night of mortal pain,
And when the morning came again,

Calmest of all his soul appears;
To give us hope, quiet our fears:
Oh! Hope so small, first to us gave,
Only one ray, this side the grave.

Oh, anguished souls, oh, tearless eyes,
Oh, hour of dread, how paralyzed
All hearts,— but lo, far o'er the sea,
From the Old World, comes sympathy.

God's messengers,— How swift they go,
To carry news of weal and woe.
O, messengers of love,—ye came,
Flying like lightning's vivid flame,—
Over the wires, at God's commands,
From sympathetic, Christian lands.

Earth's crowned heads and potentates,
Sent words of cheer,— to bar the gates,
Of death!—to bear our chieftain up.—
Oh, to assuage Woe's bitter cup.

Omen of good, to mortal sight;
Dispelling shades of coming night;
May freedom lend a brighter ray,
For those who lead her hosts to-day,
While all bow down and humbly own,
Jehovah reigns!—His will be done.

Live, manly soul, battling for life,
Comes from the homes of all the free.
The world awaits this great, grand strife;
And countless millions yet to be,
Shall rise to read, and bless thy name,
Enrolled upon the lists of fame.

A Hymn from the 96th Psalm.

Sing to the Lord a new-made song;
    O, all ye people of the earth,
Loud shout and let your praise prolong,
    Those joyful sounds of heavenly birth.

Sing unto Him, and praise His name,
    By whom we're kept from day to day;
And to the heathen, dark, proclaim,
    His glory in your heavenly lay.

His glory sing, His wonders tell,
    Displayed in Heaven, in earth, in air,
Thy holy joy, our bosoms swell,
    While we a new-made song prepare.

Honor, and strength, and majesty,
    To Father, Son and Holy Ghost,
Pour forth with heavenly minstrelsy,
    Our songs of praise delightful, most.

Ye Heavens rejoice, and earth of rock,
    And hill and dale and mountain form;
And burning fires of earthquake shock,
    And ye aloud, O, tempest storm.

Thou waving sea, be glad, rejoice,
    And lift in praise your billows high,
With thunder roar or hollow voice,
    With fearful gale or rippling sigh.

Sing to the Lord a new-made song,
And bless Him for His holiness;
And let it sweetly flow along,
Up to His throne of heavenly grace.

December, 1842.

Life is Short.

Life is short and time is fleeting,
  Soon the day of life is fled,
Soon each heart now proudly beating,
  Will lie numbered with the dead.

Precious moments, swiftly flying,
  Linger not with us to stay,
But bear us on, living or dying,
  To the spirit land away.

Oh, how transient is life's morning,
  Faded soon is beauty's bloom;
And manhood, in its glorious dawning,
  Shrouded for the silent tomb.

And old age, with locks all hoary,
  Tottering ready for its fall;
Short is Life. Oh, short is glory,
  Short is most for each and all.

Published in Vermont Christian Messenger, Feb. 26, 1854.

The Tolling Bell.

    Hear ye the tolling bell?
How mournfully it peals, how sad and slow!
Death has hurled his dart, another is laid low;
    Has bid to earth, farewell.

    Another mortal's gone,
Is numbered with the silent, sleeping dead;
The spirit, freed, hath taken wings and fled
    Where we are hastening on.

    How short our life below;
How soon our days are past, our journey o'er;
Each one and all to reach that distant shore,
    How swiftly on we go.

    O, swiftly on we glide,
Unconsciously adown Time's rapid stream.
Until at last upon our visions gleam,
    The eternal portals, wide.

    Hear'st thou the tolling bell?
Mortal? Oh! it will toll for thee, for me;
Perchance to-morrow—to-morrow it may be,
    Or sooner, none can tell.

Pub. G. M. F., Feb. 1854.

Song for Winter.

Now Winter is with us again,
   His mantle about us is spread;
No flowers of Summer remain
   To tell of the fragrance they shed.
The voices of Nature are still,
   Her minstrels are shrouded in gloom;
The valley, the meadow and hill,
   No longer appear in their bloom.

The forest is leafless and sad,
   The grove is deserted and lone;
There's nothing to make the heart glad,
   Since music of Summer is gone.
The storm-clouds are out in the sky,
   The tempest is howling around;
With fetters which seem to defy,
   The Ice King the rivers hath bound.

How gloomy the prospect appears,
   How cheerless the scenery to me;
Lo, Nature is silent, in tears,—
   In bondage, she sighs to be free.
The squirrel and bee are at rest,
   Domestics are gathered in fold;
Sure nothing unsheltered were blest,
   To perish or starve in the cold.

How merrily tinkle the bells,
   Full many a starry, cold night;

While passing the valleys and hills,
  The coursers speed on in their flight.
With rapture each bosom now swells,
  The spirit so light and so free;
The maidens are musical bells,
  So blithesome and merry are they.

Yet Winter, Oh, Winter we sigh,
  With Nature again to be free;
O, speed thee, O, hasten and fly,
  We'll gladly say farewell to thee.
For brighter and fairer is Spring,
  Its sunshine more dear to our heart;
Then hasten on readiest wing,
  And from us in kindness depart.

The Name of Morse.

The name of Morse shall live for aye.
  Lo, telegram, "What hath God wrought,"
First thrilled along the trembling wires,
  By spark of electricity.
  And heaven and earth have made reply;—
Which all the world with faith inspires;—
  Proclaims, "Live on, thou germ of thought,—
Immortal name,— shall never die."

Funeral Hymn

O, yes thy spirit now hath gone;
   Thy soul from earth hath fled;
Upon the wings of angels borne,
   To its triumphant Head.

From sin and sorrow, pain and death,
   Thou art forever free;
We saw Thee gasp thy latest breath,
   We sighing, mournfully.

Great God, impart to us thy grace,
   And make our hearts to feel,
So we may humbly seek thy face,
   Before Thee humbly kneel.

And when our work on earth is done,
   And we to death are given;
Pardon receive from thy dear Son,
   And find a home in heaven.

   Hymn composed by myself, copied off and written for the funeral of my father and sung on that occasion.
   November, 1841.

From Earth I Soared Away.

From earth I soared away,
    On Fancy's borrowed wings,
Up to the realms of day,
    Where joy eternal springs.

'Twas there I saw the blest,
    And saints and angels high;
Forever at their rest,
    Where Pain and Sorrow fly.

Nor yet are they at rest,
    Forever beaming bright,
They lean upon His breast
    Whose robes are purely white.

And fall at Jesus' feet,
    And sing the song of love;
Harmoniously sweet,
    The anthem swells above.

Through Heaven it sweetly rolls,
    And mingles with the light,
Which crowns immortal souls,
    And makes them purely white.

I saw the streets of gold,
    And walls of jasper there,
And spotless hosts unfold
    Victorious palms, they bear.

Have

Thou pass'd the pearly gates,
   Forever now at home;
No more with loves and hates,
   A world of sin to roam.

And yet the crowning Light,
   Upon His throne I see;
Dazzling with splendor bright,—
   All immortality.

Too bright for mortal gaze,
   I left the courts above;
Still list'ning to the lays,
   And wond'ring at such love.

December, 1845.

The Bobolink.

The bobolink is merry,
A merry fellow he;
He sings with joyful glee,
    Lo-pit-I-kit-ti-e-r-ry,
    Lo-kit-lo-kit-lo-kee.

He bathes his wings in sunlight,
He hovers o'er the flow'rs;
And warbles his sweet chorus,
Through all the blissful hours,
    Lo-pit-lo-kit-ti-e-r-ry,
    Lo-kit-lo-kit-lo-kee.

Down in the meadow yonder,
He sports all royally;
He frolics in the clover,
And plays the cooing lover.
    Sings lo-pit-ti-kit-ti-e-r-ry,
    Lo-kit-lo-kit-lo-kee.

A funny feathered fellow,
So comical to see;
Black, white, red and yellow,
He sings all gay and free,
    Lo-pit-lo-pit-ti-e-r-ry,
    Lo-pit-lo-kit-lo-kee.

He's happy 'mong the roses,
Sweet June's his holiday;

He soon will leave the posies,
With wifey fly away,

Down to the sunny Southland,
Through winter there to stay;
The jolly bob-o-link-tum,
And then return in May,—
  Singing his lo-pit-lo-pit-ti-e-r-ry,
  Lo-kit-lo-kit-lo-kee. ⸘

Scraps.

See proud Majestic cleave the waves;
 The broad Atlantic swiftly o'er:
In six days time,— or less,— no more,—
 From land to land, from shore to shore.⸘

The cable grapples Ocean's caves.
 And rests on Mermaid's hidden graves.
Or shallow seas its bosom laves; —
 Beneath the billowy, briny waves. ⸘

" 'Tis sweet to be remembered,"
 When all without is drear;
True friendship is a treasure,
 A blessing ever dear.

Zack and I.

Zack and I went a hunting.
>Zack and I.

With my gun upon my shoulder,
>Zack and I.

Zack he was a famous hunter,
>Zackary.
>(Good while, I guess).

He was named after General Taylor,
>So was I.

Soon we found the festive squirrel,
>Chipperi.

How he chittered, how he chattered,
How he scratched and played his antics,
>Chipperi.

O, the funny little squirrel,
Laying in his precious store;
Filled his chops with little nutties,
Then skipping back to find some more.
>Chipperi.

So we left him in his glory,
>Chipperi.

Let him tell rest of the story.
>Chipperi.

Famous hunters, homeward scampered;
>Zack and I.

Snow.

Snow, snow, snow, with a whiff, and with a wheeze;
Something of a breeze, or a regular blizzard.!
O! who can know, who is there can tell,
Why it came or fell?   Either a witch or wizard!
Damp, cold, damp, the weather has spells,
Now take off the bells, no longer can they jingle.!
Tramp, tramp, tramp, now take off the shoes, the nags
    would lose,
And shovel out with a shingle.!

    Snow, snow, snow,
Man's patience it goads, it blocks up the roads,
    Where before it had drifted.
    Time to plough. !
And yet it comes down on country and town,
    With pure wantonness gifted.!
    Toot, toot, toot,
Now blow out your wrath, to clear away path,
    For the engine's bulldozing, !
With whistle and steam, with war-whoop and scream,
    To bunt out the snow-zing. !
    Mail, mail, mail,
Neither came or went, to any one,— gent,
    Or feminine gender. !
Ho! rain, hail, don't be too polite,
    To Misses Snow-White, for she's out on a bender.!

Mourn.

Mourn for our hero dead,—
Mourn for the Nation's head,—
Mourn for the hope that's fled!

Weep, weep,— if tears can flow,
Oh, weep in bitter woe,—
One noble is laid low.

By an assassin's hand.
Bow down, oh, stricken land,—
In awful silence,— grand!

Oh, put thou sackcloth on,
For him, our chosen one,
Lament his work undone!

Cease, cease, O, busy strife,
The Nation's pale with grief,—
The world has lost a life!

From homes of all the free,
Ascends, O, God, to thee,
A wail of agony.

'Mid dirges muffled deep,
We bear him to his sleep,
While freedom's angels weep!

A martyr's crown of glory bright,
　Chieftain, is waiting now for thee.
Thou battled nobly for the right;
And countless millions yet to be,
Shall rise to read, and bless thy name,
Enrolled upon the lists of fame.

Reliance on Heaven.

Another day has passed away,
　And yet I find me here;
Life's stormy sea still sailing on,
　Where dangers thick appear.

The gather'd storms fall thick and fast,
　The winds a tempest blow;
O, shall I then my anchor cast,
　Or shall I onward go?

I'll speed my way though darkness reigns;
　Though mighty billows roll;
Though thunder-car and lightning-train,
　Pierce Nature to her soul.

The star of hope my eye shall view,
　I ne'er will give it o'er;
Sure it will guide me safely through,
　To Heaven's peaceful shore.

January, 1844.

Flowers.

Ye flowers that now with beauty bloom,
   And shed sweet fragrance 'round;
Ye soon will find an early tomb,
   For ye are of the dust.

The opening bud that with the morn,
   Unfolds its leaves to us;
Blooms for awhile, and though new-born,
   Must soon return to dust.

Ye sweetest flowers, of brightest hues,
   Most odorous and sweet;
Who can to you on earth refuse,
   And trample under feet.

Who can to you on earth deny,
   That in fair Nature's fields,
You wear the diadem,—a die
   Of all creation yields.

O, bloom ye then bright flowers, sweet flowers,
   With beauty and perfume;—
Ye zephyrs soft, refreshing showers,
   In lovely month of June.

Ye're gathering laurels for the tomb,
   And soon ye, too, must die;
Yet some, perchance, we know not whom,
   May first beneath you lie.

1844.

Almost Eight.

Almost eight, rather late
   To get up in the morning,
For all day, O, don't lay
   So late, bad habits forming.

But arouse, from your drowse,
   E'en while the morning breezes,
Blowing soft, sigh aloft,
   Among the forest treeses.

Ope your eyes, wake, arise,
   E'en while the zephyrs breathing,
On the air, sweetly there,
   A flow'ret garland's wreathing.

Wake and view, ever new,
   The beauties of the morning.
See daylight, scatter night,
   Of the day giving warning.

Gems.

Gems there are of this fair earth; —
Gems of almost priceless worth, —
Glittering 'mong the dross of earth.

Doubt and Fear.

O, gloomy Doubt and dismal Fear,
    That writhes with agony,
The heart of him, within whose ear,
    'Tis all uncertainty.

You near together are allied,
    Together mostly act,
Most cautious view the soul that's tried,
    And cunningly attack.

Doubt, with a tale as false as fair,
    Would fain make us believe
That we are wrong, and must take care
    What we for faith receive.

While Fear, awak'ned by that Doubt,
    That has on us got hold;
Makes us to shake and reel about,—
    That wily thing of old.

When in the garden Mother Eve
    Was placed by her God;
He told that she must not grieve,—
    If so, must feel the rod.

With syren tongue and soothing song;
    Most archly was beset;
And doubting, whether right or wrong,
    Was caught in that sly net.

Then Fear began to act her part,
    And quickly on the heels
Of doubt, she trod, and in the heart
    Now shook like thunder peals.

By way of Doubt, that o'er her drew
    Her shadowed mantle there;
By way of Fear, that wretched threw
    Her deep into Despair, —

She found at last she had been led
    To see the wickedness,
These knaves had done, and Conscious stung,
    Then grieved in wretchedness.

Of Doubt, that in the times of old,
    With falsehood made believe,
That into bondage, all men sold —
    The progeny of Eve.

O, Fear, most dreadful, that did sting,
    Awful with sensation,
The heart of Eve,— of Death the King
    Over all creation.

O, Doubt and Fear from me depart,
    No longer be your stay;
But let bright Hope beam on my heart,
    To cheer me on my way.

Return of May, 1844.

We welcome thee, returning May,
  Thou lovely daughter of the Spring;
We welcome thee this holiday,
  For thou dost joy and gladness bring.

Blest health is on thy blooming cheek,
  And youth and beauty in thine eyes;
Ah, lovely maiden, mild and meek,
  Thou art a child of Paradise.

And thou hast come our earth to bless,
  With fairy breeze, refreshing showers;
With all thy beauties, numberless,
  To beautify this earth of ours.

Sweet music breathes on every gale,
  Creation's chorus joins the lay;
All welcome thee and gladly hail,
  Again thy smiles, returning May.

Ere the sun, has begun
  To light with golden beaming;
Soon as a ray of opening day,
  Is on the hillside streaming.

Slumber break, stir, awake!
  While on thy cheek is glowing,
Blooming health, greatest wealth,
  That life's on thee bestowing.

Let not sleep drowsy keep,
    Thee on thy pallet snoozing;
Early rise, seize the prize,
    And see the day's dawn and closing.

Repeal.

Repeal, repeal, oh! far and wide,
    Let hill and valley ring;
Repeal, repeal, each mountain side,
    Sends back its echoing.

Our happy homes, no longer free,
    For those who hither fly;
That they may taste sweet liberty;
    Repeal, repeal the cry.

What though but scorn our prayer may meet,
    Petition,—cry repeal;
'Till thunder shakes the Judgment Seat,
    And legislators kneel.

For liberty, unmoved by awe,
    Let sober reason speak;
And doomed shall be the odious law,
    Which makes blest freedom weep.

The New Year.

A bright New Year has come again,
    How light he trips along;
He lists not to the wild wind's roar,
    Nor to the merry song.

He flies o'er the mountain, hill and dale,
    He enters every door;
Upon his face the mystic veil,
    He from the Old Year tore.

"My time has come," the Old Year said,
    "My last day now is o'er;
So take thou this of crimson red,
    And wear it as I wore."

"The eyes of man shall strive in vain,
    To read thy changeful face;
Wear it as in the days of yore,
    The eldest of our race."

And thus the New Year comes again,
    How light he trips along;
He lists not to the wild wind's roar,
    Nor to the merry song.

November.

November is a gloomy month,
   Yet beauty in its gloom;
Though Nature's sweets have most decayed,
   And found an early tomb.

There's gloom upon the forest trees,
   With mourning they are clad,
And nothing in the dismal scene
   To cheer or make them glad.

There's gloom upon the mountain top,
   And gloom within the valley;
And there is gloom in moaning winds,
   When they around us rally.

Ther'es gloom when tempest-clouds and storms
   With violence are driven;
And whirlwinds feel the biting lash,
   Of the charioteers of Heaven.

November is a gloomy month,
   Yet beauty in its gloom;
Though Nature's sweets have most decayed,
   And found an early tomb.

There's beauty in the moonlight eve,
   When stars are shining bright;
And all the host of Heaven appear,
   Refulgent with their light.

'Tis then I love to wander out,
  Their loveliness to see;
And view the glowing splendors,— light,
  The vault of Heaven's canopy.

A pure and steady light they burn.
  A flame of living light;
While every orb helps constitute
  The diadem of night.

November is a gloomy month,
  Yet beauty 'mid its gloom;
Though Nature's sweets have most decayed,
  And found an early tomb.

Joy and Sadness.

Joy and Sadness, Grief and Gladness,
  Are combined together;
Our Hope in One, bright as the sun,
  Is banished by the other.

My Father and Mother.

My father and mother have gone to their rest;
And found as we hope a home with the blest;
From sorrow and sighing, forever are free,
In the blessed abodes of eternity.

My dearest, good mother, was the first one to go,
On her brow was the paleness, on her cheek the hectic glow;
She saw that consumption was wasting away,
Yet breath'd not a prayer here longer to stay.

But calmly, when death was wasting her form,
With composure prepared, for a fairer, brighter morn.
When her time had come, and her spirit had fled,
With hope in her soul, she slept with the dead.

After years had elaps'd, my father laid down,
A wearysome burden for an immortal crown.
Long wearysome watchings, of sorrow and pain,
Were his to endure, until Death, the conquerer came.

They have passed through a world of troubles and cares;
And leave us, their children, to encounter its snares;
Their counsel we know, for often 'twas given,
Let wisdom on earth direct you to Heaven.

Farewell, then, dear parents, your sufferings are o'er;
Nor would we recall you, from Heaven's bright shore.
No, rather in silence, in solitude weep,
While you each are embalmed in memory deep.

O! farewell, but ever may you live in our heart,
Till we, from from this world so fading, depart.
And then may our spirits, o'erflowing with love,
Eternally mingle, in union above.

April, 1845.

Could We But Know.

Could we but know, or could we see,
Our lot on earth,— what is to be,—
Would it more joy, or sorrow give?
Despair, the most, or faith to live?

O, joyous is the heart, or sad;
Despondent,— or 'tis light and glad;—
With hope to cheer us on our way;
Yet looking for a brighter day.

O, but for hope our heart would break,—
So 'twas the tongue of mortal spake,
In olden time,— is it not true
Of each and all, myself and you?

No wish or thought, no eye can see,
The future of Eternity.
Oh, only Hope and Faith, sublime,
Can soar beyond the bounds of Time.

Late Poem.

Memorial Hymn.
(Bedeck their graves.)

Bedeck their graves with choicest flow'rs,
 The sweetest flow'rs of Spring;
In these sublime and pensive hours,
 Our tribute here we bring.

Sad mother, weep thy absent one,
 Sister, thy brother dear;
Proud father, o'er thy noble son,
 Let fall thy manly tear.

CHORUS.

The Union forever, cemented with blood;
May nothing it sever, O, merciful God.

For oh! they bade their country live,
 In Freedom's darkest hour,
And in their death, they to it gave,
 A great and glorious dow'r.

Dark was the morn, and dark the day;
 The nation clad in woe;
When her foul stain, was washed away,
 In their life-blood's crimson flow.

CHORUS.

The Union forever, cemented with blood;
May nothing it sever, O, merciful God.

Sleep on, O, noble heroes, sleep;
 Ye lov'd and tried and true;

While Freedom's sons shall come and weep,
    A nation's love for you;

And strew the sweetest flowers of Spring,
    Upon each soldier's grave;
Who gave his life an offering,
    Our glorious land to save.

CHORUS.

The Union forever, cemented with blood;
May nothing it sever, O, merciful God.

Composed 1871 or 1872.

Death.

Stern Death is on our track,
    Though noiseless he may be;
Whatever windings we may make,
    We cannot from him flee.

In Pleasure's flowery road,
    In Folly's blinding way;
In Virtue's paths, by many trod,
    He follows silently.

And though we see him not,
    Nor can his footsteps hear,
We shall be his, for 'tis our lot,
    To grace his sable bier.

Waiting for the Rain.

Waiting, waiting, waiting,
    Waiting for the rain.
It seems as though it never
    Would bless our homes again.

Scorching the lurid sunshine,
    On valley, hill and plain;
These drouthy days of summer,
    With languor on their train.

Sultry the air, and fitful,
    The winds that sigh in vain;
We look, and wait, and murmur,
    Of blasted hopes again.

Each tree, and leaf, and flower,
    Or what of them remain,
Invoke a potent shower,
    To bless each germ again.

Waiting, hoping, trusting,
    Despairing, yet not slain,
All life is thirsting, praying,
    For the cool, life-giving rain.!

Composed 1875, or near, severe drouth.

A Hymn of Praise and Invocation.

O! God, to thee I bend the knee,
   To thee I humbly own
Obedient bow, and worship now
   The Lord upon His throne.!

Another day has passed away,
   And now the night comes on;
Thy pow'r has kept, while time has reapt,
   And Death his work has done.

O! may I be thankful to Thee
   For all thy mercies shown;
My sins forgive, and may I live
   Nearer thy great white throne?

My pray'r is said, and on my bed
   I lay me down to rest;
O, safely keep, while I do sleep,
   And fold me to thy breast.?

And when the light dispels the night,
   And reds the morning skies;
May I anew, my way pursue,—
   My journey to the skies.!

January, 1844.

Illinois.

There is a State out in the West,
    Close nestling by Mississippi's side;—
By Nature and by man 'tis blest,
    With fields magnificent and wide,
And would you know her name, my boy?
It is our glorious Illinois.

'Tis but of late the red man trod,
    Among the wild flowers in their bloom,
And swiftly o'er her virgin sod,
    The deer was chased and met his doom,
By warrior brave and Indian boy,
Along the shores of Illinois.

And o'er her prairies, broad and free,
    The buffalo did graze and roam.
Where now the golden grain we see, —
    . Where now we find a pleasant home;
And glad to speak with pride and joy,
The glorious name of Illinois.

All honor to the men who came,
    The bold and hardy pioneers;
With hands and hearts, to till and tame,—
    The way prepare for coming years.
Three cheers for them, three cheers, my boy,
The pioneers of Illinois.

Go, farmer, follow up the plow,
    And plant with care the willing soil;
Plant trees as well as corn, and vow
    'Tis not thy mission to destroy;
But rather elevate, my boy,
The glorious name of Illinois.

And while our tribute here we pay,
    To those who've come and gone before;
Arise! Majestic, lead the way,
    O, Prairie State, forevermore,
The Empire State may bear, my boy,
    The glorious name of Illinois.

Strains Divine.

Strains divine, peal'd forth anew,
And on the wings of cherubs flew,
    Up to Heaven.

Stern Winter Reigns.

Stern Winter reigns, triumphant now,
    And spreads his wings abroad;
He pays his yearly, snowy vow,
    And Heavenward, points to God.

May.

One year ago we welcomed thee,
And now again thy beauty see.
Behold again thy loveliness,
Which does the eyes of millions bless.

And fain with harp of merry string,
Would of thy graces gladly sing.
And what, has May returned again,
To robe in green the fruitful plain?

And hill and valley, high and low,
Say, of her comings do you know?
O, yes, for flowers are on her brow,
And shed their fragrance o'er us now.

And springing fresh within our vales,
They listen to the merry tales
Of thousand songsters as they sing,
And float away on airy wing.

Ask of her coming, do you know,
When such music forth doth flow.
We tell you nothing else to-day,
Could cause such joy as youthful May

Then joy awake within my heart,
And let me take some humble part,
While all creation sweetly sings,
And claps for joy her thousand wings.

Thy breath, O, Spring, we did inhale,
And life and health we did inhale,
When first the ray of morning broke,
And things inanimate awoke.

'Twas then the stately forest old
Stood forth, its presence to unfold;
Bright beaming like a ray of truth,
In all the innocence of youth.

And thus she stood, welcome that day,
The wintry storms had passed away.
Her eternal years and hoary age
Had fled before a brighter page.

The shades of death far from her fly,
While she whispers joyfully:
Come lovely songsters to my bow'rs,
Come and deck me, fragrant flowers,
For youth and beauty, all combine,
A wreath of laurel to entwine.

Then next in place stood they of song,
To share the bliss which seemed so young,
And forth outright with merry glee
They poured their sweetest minstrelsy.

And thus they sang with gladsome notes
And music, made from mellow throats:
Up now, ye flowers, and view the morn,
Behold the millions yet unborn;

Come forth and blossom, fragrance shed,
No longer deem we all are dead.

Join in the song and swell the theme;
Awake, and view the morning's beam;
Arise, and see the forest gleam,
And know that Nature doth redeem,
From sleep and death, from wintry clime,
And bringeth back the blest Springtime.

'Twas thus the flowers made their reply:
We gladly hear your melody,
We thank you for your kind invite,
And hope we soon shall bless your sight;
And shed our fragrance on the air,
And greet the song that's swelling there.

We love the Spring, its rocks and vales,
Its hills and valleys, verdant dales.
We love its sunlight, bright and clear,
We love the freshness of its air.
We love to look from woodlands green,
And all the spacious room between.

We love the sounds of joyous mirth,
Waking o'er the radiant earth.
We like to hear the cascade's fall,
And waters to each other call.
We love the song all Nature sings:
Hosannah to the King of Kings.

May, 1845.

Speak Kindly.

Speak kindly to each other,
  Speak with all loving kindness;
And remember that thy brother
  Sees best thy own deep blindness.

All sometimes are in error;
  And some are faulty often.
Speak kindly to each other;
  For harsh words cannot soften.

Speak kindly and forgiving,
  For words in anger spoken,
Forever they are living;
  When tender ties are broken.

Speak kindly to thy neighbor;
  He sees not his own weakness.
Speak kindly, for peace labor,—
  Thy duty, in all meekness.

Speak kindly; full of sorrows,
  Are the hearts of many others;
Aid and cheer them, for to-morrow,
  Thou may'st need from thy brothers.

Speak kindly;—full of frailty
  Are we all;—unless forgiving,
Can we, poor and erring mortals,
  Hope to meet at last in Heaven?

Tears.

Who hath not known their worth?
They often bring relief
To hearts when full of grief,
To the sorrowing ones of earth,
They often bring relief.

Be not ashamed to weep.
Down let the tear-drops roll.
The anguish of the soul,
They tell how strong and deep,
They tell how strong and deep,
Down let the tear-drops roll.

They are the Spirit's friend.
Then let them fill the eye,
And chase away the sigh
That doth with anguish rend;
That doth with anguish rend;
Then let them fill the eye.

Sparkling like dewy gems,
They bless us ere we know.
They soften human woe.
Richer than diadems,
Richer than diadems,
They bless us ere we know.

Who would without them be?
Mortal, could'st thou not weep,
Thy joys and sorrows deep,
What would become of thee?
What would become of thee,
Mortal, could'st thou not weep?

Through them we look to Heaven.
In answer to our prayer,
Hoping for mercy there,
We read our sins forgiven;
We read our sins forgiven;
In answer to our prayer.

The Poor.

The poor, oh, they are many,
   And scattered far and wide;
They dwell among the mountains,
   And by the ocean's tide.

They live by plain and river,
   They throng the busy street,
And many are the noble hearts
   Which in their bosoms beat.

They build not costly houses,
   Nor Mammon is their God;
They live in little cottages,
   Their sweat bedews the sod.

Theirs are the hands that labor,
   To earn their daily bread;
Without a downy pillow,
   On which to lay their head.

Without the ease and comfort,
   The rich so much possess;
Who sooner will oppress them,
   Than comfort, love and bless.

They toil and strive and struggle,
   With poverty and care;
And many are the hardships
   They meet and meekly bear.

Though sometimes they may murmur,
    So hard their earthly lot;
And strive to live as honest,
    Though change it they may not.

And theirs are hidden sorrows,
    No human heart can know;
O, many are the secret tears,
    Which from their fountains flow.

Though they may know contentment,
    More than the wealthy, far;
Who live in costly splendor,
    With naught but wealth to mar.

Though small their earthly treasure,
    More honest they may be,
Than they who scorn them for their lot,
    And roll in luxury.

And Heaven may be nearer,
    Their hope's bright glorious home;
Where they may dwell forever,
    Where Mammon cannot come.

All Nature Sings.

All Nature sings;
Its chorus rings,
While echo brings
Upon its wings
Sublimest things.

I hear its voice;
It bids rejoice
With ceaseless noise;
And O, what toys,
Presents its joys!

Its do, la, se,
Singeth to me;
And land and sea
Are full of glee;
O, bend the knee.

O, one and all,
Down let us fall;
For from this ball
Its voice doth call,—
Behold and fall.

A Sister's Dying Farewell.

Farewell, my friends, farewell, I go;
But let no tear of sorrow flow;
Mourn not for me, O, do not weep,
When calmly I shall fall asleep,
When gently death shall close my eyes,
To ope again in Paradise.

This world is beautiful, 'tis true,
Of light and shade, and youth and bloom;
And now I go away to view
A fairer one beyond the tomb,
Whose beauties bright shall ever be
Illuming long Eternity.

Farewell, ye woods, ye birds, ye flowers,
Ye cooling shades, refreshing showers,
Ye hills and dales and mountain forms,
Ye moaning winds, ye tempest storms;
No more of you my senses tell;
But, oh, 'tis hard to say farewell!

Rocks, founts and rills, and flowing streams,
Ye balmy airs and morning beams,
Ye clouds and skies, and day and night,
Ye morn and eve, with beauty bright,
Sun, moon and stars, and mournful knell,
I now must bid you all farewell.

Farewell, my home, my native hearth,
To me the dearest spot on earth.
Adieu, vain hope and fleeting time;
I leave you for a fairer clime.
Ye holy days and Sabbath bell,
Much have I loved you — long and well.

That brighter world breaks on my view;
My suff'rings o'er, my journey through.
Ye angel bands, my spirit bear,
Far from this world of pain and care.
Ye friends and scenes I've loved so well,
With joy I breathe a last farewell.

Acrostic.

ORPHA SHIPMAN.

O Calvary, 'tis oft I think of thee.
Red with bloody, dying agony;
Put on my soul thy own immortal light,
Hushed in deep awe, yet trembling at the sight,
An ashy paleness settles on thy brow.

Savior, Redeemer, and Lord, but Thou
Hast strength thy dying agony to bear.
In answer to thy last imploring prayer,
Prayer offered up, but not for strength alone,
My god forgive them, blent with every groan.
Ages have fled, that prayer for thee, for me,
Ne'er dies, but lives with scenes of Calvary.

Spring.

O, gentle Spring, thou hast returned once more;
The Winter's past, his dismal reign is o'er,
And thou hast come with song and light and flowers,
With sunshine, soft blue skies, refreshing showers.
The gushing founts, unfettered now and free,
Are leaping forth in all their merry glee.

The brooks again, full of their pleasing tales,
Go tattling on through newly flower'd vales.
The grass springs forth, all bright and green again,
All beautiful, from valley, hill and plain.
A carpet soft for mortal feet is spread,
All decked with gems in colors bright arrayed.

The dandelion rears its head of gold;
The violets meek, their tiny leaves unfold.
Forth from their homes the merry children stray;
New treasures find, each warm and sunny day.
The herds are out upon the verdant hills,
And lambkins sport around the sparkling rills.

Again the woods put on their leafy bloom,
And verdure springs from last year's early tomb.
The husbandman resumes his welcome toil,
And seeds with willing hands the precious soil.
The feathered tribes, O, Spring, return with thee;
And fill the air with their sweet minstrelsy.

Sweet is the song, O, sweet the matin lay,
Which ushers in each new, succeeding day!
Faith, Hope and Joy, expectant now arise,
And mingle with the music of the skies.
Welcome, sweet Spring, in all thy youthful bloom,
Thrice welcome in thy Nature's happy home.

Is there a Day without a Morn?

Is there a day without a morn?
Is there a rose without a thorn?
Is there a hope without a fear?
Is there a smile without a tear?

Is there a night without an end?
Oh! who would live without a friend?
Is anyone without their woes?—
We search in vain for a thornless rose.

Is there a bliss without a sigh?—
O, all the living, sure, must die.
Is there a face so sweet and fair,
But leaves a trace of sorrow there?

O, are there lips but what have pressed
A blessing on a mother's breast?
O, sad the heart without a friend,
O! life immortal, cannot end.

Late Poem.

There's Beauty but It Fades Away.

There's beauty in the blushing morning,
　But it soon fades away.
There's beauty in the lovely evening,
　But it soon fades away.

There's beauty in the blooming flower,
　But it soon fades away.
There's beauty in the rainbow shower,
　But it soon fades away.

There's beauty on the sunlit mountain,
　But it soon fades away.
There's beauty in the sparkling fountain,
　But it soon fades away.

There's beauty in the flowing river,
　But it soon fades away.
There's beauty in the leaves that quiver,
　But it soon fades away.

There's beauty in the foaming billows,
　But it soon fades away.
There's beauty in the weeping willows,
　But it soon fades away.

There's beauty in the seasons vernal,
　But it soon fades away.
There's beauty in things eternal,
　But it soon fades away.

There's beauty in the lovely Springtime,
   But it soon fades away.
There's beauty in the golden Autumn,
   But it soon fades away.

There's beauty in the vernal Summer,
   But it soon fades away.
There's beauty in the hoary Winter,
   But it soon fades away.

There's beauty in our early childhood,
   But it soon fades away.
There's beauty in our glorious manhood,
   But it soon fades away.

But there is a beauty that does not fade,
   'Tis away in yonder Heaven.
On the Savior our burden was laid,
   His life for us was given.

Spring Appears.

'Neath April's genial sky
The golden sunbeams lie,
The clouds of darkness fly,
    And beauty reigns.

The Winter winds have gone,
On wings away have flown,
No more their tempest tone
    Is heard around.

The buds of Spring appear,
And soon will blossom here,
The heart of man to cheer,
    Nature most fair.

For 'scaped her wint'ry tomb,
With all its dismal gloom,
She comes in youthful bloom,
    And sweetly smiles.

And joy and hope are there,
And fill the balmy air,
With incense sweet as prayer,
    Then rise above.

All nature sweetly sings,
And claps her thousand wings,
Creation's chorus rings,
    And tells of God.

1844.

Grant.

The war-clouds had gathered
 In our country's sky;
And traitors had threatened
 To ruin or die;

Our flag had insulted,
 And trampled in dust;
By our forefathers bequeathed
 A great, sacred trust.

And Sumpter had spoken,
 'Mid flame and 'mid smoke,
With cannon's loud thunder,
 And the whole land awoke

With terror and with anguish,
 With fear and with gloom;
The struggle commenced,
 The contest had come;

And the blood of the Union,
 Of our sons and our sires,
Was kindled, and mingled
 In the battle's fierce fires.

Bull Run was enacted,
 With its hasty retreat;
Then followed disaster,
 Dismay and defeat;

Our leaders all failed
   To conquer the foe;
And the Union bewailed
   Its heroes laid low.

Then Heaven smiled and gave us
   A leader, who came
To the front of the battle,
   And GRANT was his name.

Yes, Heaven smiled and gave us
Our brave, good Ulysses,
   The loyal and true;
To lead us and save us,
   With the boys in blue.

How he planned, how he fought
   The foemen so well,
Let Henry and Donelson
   His strategy tell.

Like the dawning of day
   O'er the darkness of night,
So our hero brought forth
   The morning of light.

And Vicksburg and Lookout,
   And Mission's red flame,
The siege, and assault,
   Made glorious his name.

In the Wilderness' struggle,
   So fierce and so long,
Where Lee with his army
   Was posted so strong;

And where the wily chieftain
   Thought to turn him back,
Grant battled for the Union,
   Nor lost he the track.

Like the children of Israel,
   In the wilderness old.
But planned in the darkness,
   And as a lion bold,

In the morning his army
   Was on its last tramp,
And flanking the foe,
   Broke ranks in his camp.

A halo of glory
   Was shining around him;—
And Richmond was doomed,—
   The last siege before him.

He came in the darkness, —
   He ushered in the day; —
He rose from lowly station,—
He led to save the Nation; —
   And war passed away.

Campaign Song.

When Treason raised its monster head,
    And sought to rend our land in twain;
Then Freedom's hosts uprose, and said,
    Our country must, and shall remain!

Oh, long and cruel was the strife;
    Oceans of blood and treasure flowed;
To save for us the Nation's life,
    Imperiled by the threat'ning sword.

Defiant first, in Congress Halls;
    Then Sumpter, pierced, and bleeding, fell.
Assailed again are Freedom's walls,—
    Oh, brothers, ponder long and well.

The dying words of martyrs heed;
    The admonitions which they gave;
Regardless now of party breed,
    Freemen, be loyal, true and brave.

Think of the fathers, brothers, lost;
    And shall the struggle come again?
Oh, God, at what a fearful cost,
    Was blotted out a Nation's shame!

Oh, heed the lessons of the past,
    The warning call, ere 'tis too late;
The dark'ning clouds their shadows cast,—
    And doom or glory us await.

True liberty throughout our land,
    And blessed peace and hope abide;
O, ye who love our country, grand,
    Guard well her honor, and her pride.

Like deaf'ning thunders in the sky,
    Like ocean's surges sweeping roar,
Shout forth the loyal battle cry:—
    Strike with the ballot's mighty power.

Presidential Campaign, 1880.

Acrostic.

SUSAN C. LOWELL.

Sweet are contentment's peaceful hours,
Unmarked, undimm'd by pain or care.
Sweet, sweet as Eden's rosy bowers,
And calm as evening-time of prayer.
Not honor, glory, fame, or wealth,

Can so impart the bloom of health.

Let sweet contentment, then, be thine;
O, sister dear,—
Watch, labor, pray;
Enter the straight and narrow way.
Live so thy end may peaceful be;
Love well thy God,— remember me.

Meter.

What kind of time in measuring rhyme,
    I leave it out to Peter;
In sacred song, is short or long,
    Mostly in use,—or common meter?

There's six, and seven, ten, and eleven
    Meter; helps out the rhyming;
But light the wear, upon the stair,
    Of pilgrims heavenward climbing.

There is a kind we often meet;
    Another, found,—of joyful sound.
We lay the crown at Jesus' feet;
Our loud hosannas there repeat;
'Tis hallelujah, long and sweet.

And one more kind, is all combined;
    'Tis slower or 'tis fleeter;
And changed to suit, each part, not mute,
    Of every form and feature.
Makes sad our song, or sweeter,—
    O, bless the Lord, and Peter!

June Training Day.

O, how I loved June training day,
    No matter what the weather;
At shriek of fife, and beating drum,
    To march and strut together.

Our captain's name, of world-wide fame,
    Was dear old Uncle Simon;
And long or short, of vague report,
    Our training on the common.

Upon parade, a tall cockade,
    An awful gaudy feather;
Our captain wore, six hours or more,
    No matter what the weather.

At nine o'clock that blessed day,
    O, what a mighty drumming;
They called the roll of every soul,
    To see if they were coming.

And then the drill, to noon until;
    Of that dear old militia;
They shouldered arms, they grounded arms,
    Then dinner, smoke — tobacco.

And then, full stout, they strutted out,
    To finish up so jolly;
Then home away, that holiday,
    And tea, with Aunty Polly.

April, 1894.

Childhood.

'Tis oft backward I turn my eyes,
   Until sweet visions crowding come;
Those scenes before me rise,
   Again I'm in my childhood's home.

Again I hear my mother's voice,
   I sit upon my father's knee,
And mine again those little toys
   I treasured in my childish glee.

Brothers and sisters there I meet,
   And playmates where we played before;
O, there's no place on earth so sweet,
   As this I loved so much of yore.

We leave again our own dear cot,
   When Spring returns with gentle showers,
And wander o'er the little plot,
   And cull among the grass, the flowers.

We wander by the pebbly brook,
   And pluck the flowers that sweetly bloom,
And trace with care each shadowy nook
   That lies around our pleasant home.

Again we tread the wildwood free,
   In Summer's warm and genial day,
Where singing bird and busy bee
   Flitter and hum around our way.

Once more we climb the hillside steep,
  Where lambkins sport by sparkling rills;
Once more the silver cascade's leap
  My youthful heart with rapture fills.

Down in the mead again we go,
  The pond, the mill, familiar seem;
The shady tree, the orchard, too;
  The bridge that crossed our own loved stream.

At eve, a happy little band,
  We gathered round the cheerful hearth;
We talked about the spirit land,
  And said how beautiful is earth.

How blissful was each varying scene,
  Sweet flowers beneath, bright stars above,
And songs of merry birds between,
  The gay, green earth, and stars we loved.

Oh, happy childhood, back to thee
  I look through years of joy and pain;
And fondly trace in memory
  The scenes I ne'er shall see again.

Where now the humble little cot
  Wherein I drew my infant breath?
Deserted, lonely and forgot,
  And as the house of Death.

And where are those who roamed with me
  The wildwood and the flowery dell?

They're some upon the broad, blue sea,
  And some to earth have bid farewell.

I wake as from a trance, — my dreams,
  The brightness of thy days has fled;
No more for me thy golden beams,
  No more among thy flowers I tread.

Adieu, I bid adieu to thee,
  While sighs my heaving bosom swell,
Farewell, so joyous, bright and free,
  I bid thee long and last farewell.

For Adam's Race.

For Adam's race of sinful man,
A full atonement made has been;
Sinners by him we all were made,
On us his sinful nature laid:
To him we trace our wretched fall,
And each are cursed, each one, and all;
Yet Jesus Christ a ransom's given,
That we may dwell at last in Heav'n.

O, in Retirement and Alone.

O, in retirement and alone
   I'd pass my time away;
Would muse on Nature's lovely scenes
   While I, a pilgrim stay.

Would pass in meditation deep
   The moments as they fly;
And would for sake of poesy,
   My powers, unknown try.

I'd gaze on scenes of beauty rare,
   Would study Nature's laws;
Would, musing, try to trace the link
   Between effect and cause.

The fields of Nature, widely spread,
   A rich repast would make;
The world celestial, and the spheres,
   Which God in being spake.

The golden sun, whose vernal rays,
   The light of every world,
Spreads light abroad, and by our God
   Was into chaos hurled.

The Heavenly spheres, whose rolling might
   Eternal in their course,
Majestic move,—to us proclaim,
   Their never-ceasing force.

From Heaven's bright arch to earth's green sod
I'd study Nature and her God;
The things of earth that upward turn,
The things of Heaven that brightly burn,
All things in sea, in earth and air,
Proclaim Almighty Power is there.

July, 1842.

Acrostic.

BETSEY JANE LOWELL.

Betsey, be good to your father and mother,
Especially to your mother be kind;
Take pains to please your brother and sister,
So shall you have peace and comfort of mind.
Employ thy time doing well — eschew evil;
Your sayings and doings take care of.

June roses are sweet and yet civil,
And remember their beauty will wear off.
Notwithstanding you're young and some witty,
Excuse me, for it was a slip of the tongue,

Lack not in well doing your duty,
O, no, though you are but little and quite young.
What a jewel is true friendship! Remember,
Enduring, and ever be it thine to share,
Like the evergreen, green in December,
Like the live-forever, green everywhere.

December, 1844.

My Mountain Home Song.

O, as fair and bright as Heaven's gay light
　　Are the places where I roam;
The air is as free as the lightning's glee
　　Around my mountain home.
　　Around my mountain home.
The air is as free as the lightning's glee
　　Around my own dear mountain home.

O, I love to dwell in the quiet dell,
　　Where the wild-flowers sweetly bloom,
Where the sparkling rills leap down from the hills
　　Of my fairy mountain home.
　　Of my fairy mountain home.
Where the sparkling rills leap down from the hills
　　Of my fairy mountain home.

O, the eagle may fly far up in the sky
　　At the hour of midsummer's noon;
Yet farther I soar at the night's starry hour
　　Within my silent mountain home.
　　Within my silent mountain home.
Yet farther I soar at the night's starry hour
　　In my silent mountain home.

Pub. G. M. F., March, 1850.

Where Shall the Poet Find a Theme?

Where shall the poet find a theme?
 In fairy tale, in pleasant dream,
In bright-winged clouds of angel form,
 And in the lightning, in the storm.

In every cup of sparkling dew,
 In every rainbow's blended hue,
In sweetest, blushing rose of June,
 In every flower of sweet perfume.

O, in the seasons as they roll
 In grandest awe from pole to pole,
In youth, in age, in manhood's prime,
 In ringing bells of sweetest chime.

In river's still, majestic flow,
 In ocean's caves, its waves below,
In thought that soars from earth away,
 Up to the realms of endless day.

In stars that glow with splendor bright,
 And crown the diademed night,
In hope, in joy, in faith sublime,
 That soar beyond the bounds of time.

April, 1894.

Our Life a Dream.

Our life is but a dream.
How few the moments seem,
As quickly down its tide
We swiftly onward glide
With visions on our way.

We're swiftly passing on,
The rolling stream upon,
Where clouds in anger frown
And thunderbolts come down,
We dash, we dash away.

'Mid storm and tempest now,
The angry Heavens bow;
Our trembling bosoms heave,
Our hearts with sorrow grieve,
We dash the tear away.

But 'tis not always so,
That thus we onward go,
In sorrow and in grief,
Without a kind relief,—
We've pleasure on our way.

With sunshine and with bliss
Beauty the skies doth kiss,
And all serenely bright,
Us on our journey light,
Make light our toilsome way.

And so it is with us—
Sometimes bless, sometimes worse;
We're all upon the tide
Of life, and swiftly glide
Away, away, away.

Extracts.

Can we forget the men of old
   Who raised the battle-cry,
Who with prophetic eye foretold
   Triumph of liberty?

Can we forget our soldiers dead,
Who for their home and country died?

Can we forget our Lincoln's fall,
Our greatest, noblest martyr slain—
The darkest crime,—darkest of all,
That can a nation's record stain?

There love her golden harp shall take
And chant immortal lays,
Shall bid each joyful tongue awake
To join the general praise.

The Cold, Chill Hand of Death.

The cold, chill hand of death
   Is resting on thy brow,
And from the scenes of this vain earth
   Thy spirit's passing now.

And now the purple tide
   Of life has ceased to flow,
No more to give to manhood's pride
   A rich and crimson glow.

Unto the Spirit Land
   Thy soul did take its flight,
While gathered here we mournful stand,
   Still bless'd with heavenly light.

Now in the silent tomb
   We lay thee down to rest,
While we remain, and pain and gloom
   Dwell in our aching breast.

O, God! on Thee we call,
   And ask for grace divine;
O, bless us now, each one and all,
   And make us wholly thine.

And may we see and feel
   Thou doest all things right;
Our sins forgive, our pardon seal,
   And keep us by thy might.

Lines composed on the death of a young man in Milford, Mass., 1842.

Ogle County in Rhyme.

'Tis but of late the Red Man trod
Among her wildflow'rs in their bloom,
And swiftly o'er her virgin sod
The deer was chased and met his doom,
By warrior brave and Indian boy,
Along the shores of Illinois.

Winnebago county on the north,
And Stevenson about one-fourth,
DeKalb is east,— on south is Lee.
Carroll on western bound we see.

Rock River runs meandering through,
Makes equal, east, and west sides, too;
Southwesterly its course is seen;
Prairies, woodlands, and hills between.

Seven towns the river lays along,
The county seat is Oregon.
Historic names appear to view,
We've Lafayette and Taylor, too.

On east side, north, Scott and Monroe,
And Marion northeast we show;
Byron on west side, Northline, plann'd,
And Maryland, our Maryland."

White Rock, Linnville, Flag and Dement,
Southeast, help fill the complement,

Except Pine Rock and Nashua,
On east side, which together lay.

Leaf River, Foreston and Brookville,
North and northwest, west side we hail,
Eagle Point, Pine Creek and Buffalo
Are in the southwest part, we know.
Rockvale, Mount Harris and Haldame *Morris*
Come in between with one new name;
The roll's complete with Grand Detour,
Making in all just twenty-four.

E. R. Morse.

The Maiden's Choice.

O, young and fair was that maiden rare,
    And her joyous spirit free
As the winds that roam 'round her mountain home,
    While sporting in their glee.

And before her lay, in bright array,
    The path in which she trod,
While the flowers sweet, beneath her feet,
    Led her thoughts ofttimes to God.

Make me your choice, said a small, still voice,
    'Twas the blessed Savior's call,
I am the light, the truth and the life,
    And the way to Heaven for all.

Give thy heart to me and I will be
    Thy guardian and thy friend,
While life shall last, and when it is past,
    Thy joys shall never end.

Then the Tempter came and laid a claim
    To that jewel bright and rare;
Maiden, said he, follow thou me,
    For the world is bright and fair.

Thy pulse beats strong, thy life will be long,
    Sweet pleasures crown thy way;
Heed not that voice, make me your choice.
    O, come thou with me away.

And thus she strove, with a creature love,
  Against the Savior's charms;
And the things of earth, of meaner worth,
  She clasped within her arms.

Then the Savior said, be not afraid,
  For I bled and died for thee;
Now come to me, come, in thy youthful bloom,
  And from all thy sins be free.

This pearl behold, nor shining gold
  Nor earthly gem can vie,
Treasure divine, make it thou thine,
  Wilt thou not not come and buy?

One thing I ask, a humble task
  Is it for thee to do,
Give me thy heart and I will impart
  This treasure unto you.

Then the maiden sought with all her heart
  The pearl of greatest price,
And ever has been contented since then
  With her high and happy choice.

Published in Vermont Christian Messenger, March 26, 1854.

It is a Shame.

It is a shame
My countrymen, world-wide and dark, that we,
With all our boastings, are not free;
Our country deals in human flesh and blood,
And tramples on the image of our God.
   Who is to blame?

It is a shame
The fairest portion of our favored land
Should wither 'neath th' oppressor's iron hand,
A with'ring curse, and evil is the hour,
Which gives to Slavery th' reins of pow'r
   In Freedom's name.

It is a shame
The dark-hued African is doomed to toil
And till for naught, himself the spoiler's spoil,
While white men revel and bless ofttimes the laws
Which statesmen make for boasted Freedom's cause,
   Though poor and lame.

It is a shame
Our patriotic Congressmen yet meet
To make our laws where Slavery holds her seat,
And then unto their fettered brethren tell
Of liberty,— boast that they love it well.
   Always the same.

It is a shame
For northern freeman to quail and cower
At Slavery's threat, oppression's boasted pow'r;
It is a shame to boast of liberty
While we ourselves uphold dark slavery.
          We are to blame.

The Heavens Thy Power Proclaim.

The heavens thy power proclaim,
The stars, a shining flame,
Shed forth their brilliant light,
Beaming with beauty bright.

A thousand orbs that shine,
The starry heavens line;
And moon, the queen of night,
That blesses us with light.

The great and brilliant sun,
That great and mighty one,
The light of every world,
Thou into chaos hurled.

Around which all things move,
Thy power and wisdom prove,
Speak thy wisdom, prove thy power
Every moment, every hour.

Come, Blooming Health.

Come, blooming health, go thou with me,
The far and lovely West to see;
Bright hopes attend,—ye prospects fair
Around me smile—the way prepare.

Farewell my home, 'mong hills enshrined,
Oft fanned by breeze of mountain wind;
Adieu! kind friends, ye sainted dead
Who in the grave I mournful laid.

But let me drop once more a tear,
O'er dust I held in life so dear;
And, kneeling on the sacred sod,
Invoke the blessing of my God.

And now I go—leave all behind,
Friends still, and those to dust confined;
Adieu, New England's mountains green,
And hills and vales smiling between.

What glorious skies! what balmy airs!
What wide-spread scenes compared to theirs.
Here blooming nature smiles around,
And says thy Paradise is found.

Go forth in all thy manhood's prime,
And reap the fruits of this fair clime;
Go, view the wilderness in bloom,
And find perchance, an early tomb.

Ah yes, the grave may wait him there,
Stern death may bid him soon prepare.
His mandate's call none can defer,
O, who can stay the Conqueror?

Or beauteous nature may prolong
This threaded life, and make it strong,
Through mercy's door, at God's behest,
In all her blooming beauties drest.

Yet no prophetic eye can know,
The future,—or its pages scan;
And thus it is with all below,—
Nor can we know the end of man.

In letter to J. K., November 19, 1846.

The Dying Christian.

My work below which I begun
Some years ago, is nearly done,
And now I go to see the Son.
    All is well.

I go to where my Savior reigns,
For he has washed my sinful stains,
And heav'n prepaid with groans and pains.
    All is well.

I've labored long, my labor's o'er;
I've suffered wrong, but will no more;
I catch the song of heaven's shore—
    All is well.

Come, friends, and see a Christian die,
Come see him close the weary eye,
Come and bid us last good-bye.
    All is well.

Come, parents dear, give me your hand;
Come brothers near, why far-off stand?
O, dry your tears, ye sister band,—
    All is well.

Weep not for me, no, dry your tears;
The king of terrors has no fears,
Nor shall he through th' eternal years.
    All is well.

Weep not for me when I am gone,
But cheerful be still journeying on,
Till victory you all have won.
    All is well.

And wandering sinner come and see
The heav'n prepared for you and me,
And happy be eternally.
    All is well.

O glory, glory! in my soul,
Salvation's waves now o'er me roll,
And make my panting spirit whole.
    All is well.

My lasting home, in heav'n, bright heav'n,
Jesus a pledge has surely giv'n;
I know my sins are all forgiv'n.
    All is well.

Farewell, farewell! My friends, farewell!
I go away in heaven to dwell;
No more to sigh, or say farewell.
    All is well.

December, 1844.

A Vermont Snow Storm.

The storm breaks forth with fury now,
    And swiftly falls the snow
Upon the mountain's cloud-top'd brow,
    And all around below.

The virgin snow comes whirling down
    Fiercely from clouds above,
That, lowering darkly, madly frown,—
    Tempestuously move.

With mantle white, old mother earth
    Is now most nicely covered;
While dances round with breezy mirth
    That which o'er her hovered.

The blanket that has on us come,
    A full foot and three inches,
Closely keeps some denn'd up at home,
    Most quiet in their trenches.

Old Boreas on the scene appears,
    And howling comes along;
He takes us by the nose and ears
    While blowing out his song.

Cuts up his shines, and whirls about,
    As if he did not care,
And roaring, blustering, most stout,
    And strides, Oh, everywhere.!

But stop and look, there shines the sun;
In your career now stop.
And now my tale, but just begun,
It'll end, and off I'll pop.

On advent of a heavy snow storm, Feb. 18, 1842, Brookfield, Vt.

Youth.

Harken, O, youth; thou hast riches greater
Than earth can bestow,–and hidden treasures
More precious than gold;–and thine is a gem
Brighter, more lustrous and of greater worth,
Than all the gems that deck an earthly crown.

These riches are the fountains of thy heart.
These treasures are the well-springs of thy joy;
And that gem,—it is thy immortal soul.

Then wander not,–but walk in wisdom's ways;
Enrich thy mind,–add to thy treasures,
Beautify thy own,–adorn it daily,—
That gem,–a germ of immortality.

To The Moon.

Ah! bright-eyed moon, thou queen of night,
Shedding thy mild and radiant light
'Mid your bright stars that glowing shine
And kiss each other at thy shrine,
Shed now thy light o'er all the scene,
While Nature's dressed in lovely green,
And on the slumbers of the night
Bless thou my longing, raptured sight.

Yes, while deep is locked in slumber
Living things of countless number,
And all creation sweetly sleeps,
With dewy tears, unconscious, weeps,
By thy soft light I'll steal away,
And humbly kneeling, tribute pay,
While thy bright beams alike are shed
O'er slumbering life and sleeping dead.

Ah! lovely is thy borrowed light,
Which thou dost shed o'er Nature's night,
Kissing the tears of grief away,
And speaking joy in every ray.
How oft from worldly care I rove,
To meet the smiles I so much love,
To muse in silence and alone,
And weep the world so cold has grown,
Aware that sorrow finds a friend,
In every charm thy graces lend.

'Tis holy, blessed and divine,
'Tis heavenly, bright and fair,
To greet a face kindly as thine,
Smiling on midnight's balmy air,
Chasing the gloom of Nature's night
Beyond the realm of beaming light.

My counselor in bygone years,
Beholder of unfailing tears,
Thou witnesser of inward grief,
Oft hast thou brought me sweet relief;
Sweeter by far than human tone,
Thy sweet and soothing voice alone.

While bygone centuries have slept,
Nightly thy watchings thou hast kept,
Hast shed thy light on every shore,
Where waters great and mighty roar;
On meadows, fields, and woods and hills,
On cloud-top'd mounts, on gushing rills,
On briny ocean's mighty deep
Thy nightly vigils thou dost keep,
Whose bright blue waves eternal roll,
And mix the center with the Pole.

Ah! now thy beams in gentle waves
Do shed mild light o'er nameless graves,
O'er beggar'd heads and mouldering kings,
Now thy proud arch its beauty flings.

And when o'er me death flings his pall,
When hushed in silence, mute is all,
Then mourner, pale shall thy soft light
Beam o'er my grave in silent night,

Shall kiss the place where 'neath I lay,
And shall the debt of tribute pay;—
A friend indeed to each and all,
Who dwell on this terrestrial ball."

Acrostic.

<small>ORRA LAPORTE.</small>

O, phrenology, thou twin sister of
Religion, when will the world of mankind
Receive thee as such,—know thee as thou art,
And learn from all thy teachings to do well?

Luther's name ornaments the historic page,
And as long as Christianity lives
Points to the Reformation, so the name
Of Gall shall not be forgotten ever,
Recorded bright on time's annals, shall not
Tarnish, but always shine a brilliant star
Europe bore, but may the world receive thee.

December, 1842.

The Parting Hour.

The parting hour, it soon will come,
    When we no more shall meet
Within these walls, as oft we've done,
    Our lessons to repeat.

We, who have passed our time away
    In study, and in thought;
We who have labored night and day,
    And faithfully have sought—

For what we came here to obtain,
    We soon, we soon must part;
Few fleeting moments yet remain,
    To bless each throbbing heart.

The tolling bell, which brings us here
    To meet at hour of prayer,
No more [illegible] and clear—
    No more to us [illegible] smile or tear.

We oft have met, but nevermore
    Together all shall be,
While we are travelers on this shore
    To vast eternity.

The time has come; farewell! we part,
    And bid a kind adieu;
We go, each youthful, throbbing heart,
    Our homes again to view.

Newberry Seminary, 1841. Winter Term.

Take The Bible For Your Guide.

Take the Bible for your guide,
Ye young and fair in beauty's pride,
A garland wreathing on your brow,
The Book of Books, O, read it now.

You're in the slippery paths of youth,
And need be guided by its truth;
O, search it then with constant care,
And God will own and bless your prayer.

Ten thousand snares lie in your way
To draw, entice and lead astray;
The tempter, arch, the world begin,
In life's seed-time, young hearts to win.

The sea of life is full of shoals,
And wave on wave in fury rolls,
And tempest-toss'd, the bark is riven,
Unless its holy light is given.

Like fragrant flowers you now may bloom,
Yet find with them an early tomb.
O, then, how sweet to yield the breath,
When full of love, no sting has death.

Take the Bible for your guide,
Ye young and fair in beauty's pride;
To God, your Maker, humbly bow,
The Book of Books. O, read it now.

O, Lightly, Softly Tread.
MEMORIAL HYMN.

O, lightly, softly tread,
   The nation mourns to-day,
Its brave, heroic dead,
   While we our tribute pay.

Come, bow the head and heart,
   Stretch forth the friendly hand;
O, peaceful be their sleep
   Who died to save our land.

O, strew ye flowers, sweet flowers,
   And let their fragrance rise,
In these sublimest hours,
   Like incense to the skies.

Let fall the pensive tear,
   And yearn each sorrowing heart;
A stricken band takes here
   With each and all a part.

O, Freedom, look and live,
   Here is thine altar found;
The living, and the dead
   Meet on this hallow'd ground,—

And swear through blood and tears,
   To guard with faithful hand,
Through all the coming years,
   Our great, our glorious land.

On the Death of Torrey.

The martyr's gone in manhood's prime,
  His work on earth is done,
He's gone to dwell in Freedom's clime,
  His crown of glory won.

Oppression could not let him stay
  In this slave land of ours,
Yet calmly went he on his way,
  Defying all its pow'rs.

For God was his in that lone cell,
  The mighty and the strong,
And said to him: "All shall be well,
  And I'll avenge thy wrong."

And lo! the prison bars are burst,
  The captive now is free;
In God he put his only trust,
  The God of liberty.

He saw, he felt his brother's woe,
  His brother bound in chains,
He acted for that brother, too,
  And suffer'd martyr's pains.

O, noble, heav'n-born melting love,
  That thus could sacrifice
That noble heart, — thus cause it weep,
  Thus sever earthly ties.

Would that its fires might kindle ours,
    And fan a heavenly flame,
Till all our higher, nobler pow'rs
    Were glowing with the same.

The martyr's gone in manhood's prime,
    His work on earth is done;
He's gone to dwell in Freedom's clime,
    His crown of glory won.

Oppressors trembling at his fall,
And dying is his fame;
Say not he sleeps beneath the pall,
    Immortal is his name.

And dearer far to Freedom's sons,
    Than riches bought with blood,
Shall shine forever bright among
    The jewels of his God.

  Published in the Green Mountain "Freeman," July 16, 1846. Torrey was imprisoned for aiding or abetting slaves to escape from their masters, in Maryland, I think, and a little while before the Fugitive Slave Law was passed.
                                                              —E. R. M.

A Light is on the Mountains.

A light is on the mountains;
    Along the mountains green
The holy fires of Freedom
    Send forth a radiant gleam.

And soon the fanning breezes
    Shall cause them brighter glow,
Till light like golden sunshine
    Is flooding all below.

Till every nook and corner
    Is filled with beamy light,
And all enlightened freemen
    Are acting in the right.

Long had their fires been burning,
    These beacon lights of old,
Yet dimly had they slumbered,
    Till they were getting cold.

But now the breeze has rous'd them,
    The breezes brisk at play,
And brightly they are glowing,
    The fires of liberty.

Ho! every one to battle,
    Come at your country's call,

Your armor girded tightly,
    Come to the rescue all.

Gather from hill and valley
    Around our mountain fires,
And let your bosoms catch it,
    As did our goodly sires.

The spirit of our fathers
    Awake within our breast;
How can we longer slumber
    While millions are oppressed?

Come all ye honest freemen,
    A strong and mighty band,
Lift up your trumpet voices
    To save a guilty land.

A mighty work's before us,
    A mighty work to do;
Then let us not prove traitors,
    But freemen bold and true.

Let no one shrink from duty,
    But grapple with the foe;
The groaning of the victims
    Comes from the land of woe.

Ye mountain fires grow brighter,
    Intenser, till the day
When routed is the monster,
    And driven far away.

And longer,—burn forever,
　　As long as time endure,
When each and all shall slumber,
　　Then burn ye bright and pure.

Calvary.

With sorrows and with grief look up,
　　And see the Savior there;
He meekly takes the bitter cup,
　　Its bitterness to share.

On Calvary's rugged, lonely brow,
　　'Twixt Heaven and earth we see,
Nailed to the cross, the Savior now
　　Writhing in agony.

His time has come, the time of death,—
　　And for a world he dies;
Unto the Godhead, yields his breath,
　　As on the cross he lies.

No wonder then the earth did quake,
　　Like mighty billows roll;
The marble rend, the mountains shake,—
　　And groan from pole to pole.

Mount Pulaski.

Pulaski, Pulaski, on thy summit I stand,
With pencil and paper just now in my hand;
My eye it is gazing on the scenery below,
The pretty little villa, the river's still flow.

In quiet and grandeur it gently reposes,
All lovely and blooming, its beauty discloses;
The churches and their spires and the houses so neat,
Of this pretty little villa are spread at my feet.

Connecticut is winding, majestic and slow,
Her waters are peaceful, to the ocean they go,
Through rich meadows and fields, in the valleys beneath,
Now flow'rs are blooming for a mantle and wreath.

The mountains of New Hampshire are lifting their heads
To clouds that seem making on their summits their beds,
Which, rolling in darkness all along their blue tops,
Heaven's dews are distilling in the blessed dewdrops.

The wind it blows chilly and the rain it descends,
So no more, my dear Willie—my description it ends;
Pulaski, farewell, and this favorite bow'r,
Where I've spent, I can't tell, perhaps a half hour.

Pulaski Mountain, in Newberry, Vermont. 1841.

They Will not Let Them Go.

They will not let them go;
But hold their brothers with an iron hand,
In boasted freedom's fair and happy land,
　　Where all should freedom know.

Proud name our country bears,
Abroad, among the nations of the world;
In every clime her starry flag's unfurled,
　　Yet this foul stain she wears.

Three million servile slaves!
Alas! sad spectacle; oh, let us weep
For this great wrong,—that justice yet doth sleep,
　　Where freedom's banner waves.

They will not let them go,—
But still their toil, and tend'rest ties devour;
Blind to their doom,—to that approaching hour,
　　Which brings their overthrow.

And yet their cry goes up,—
While every tear their greatest want makes known
And every sigh, reaches their Father's throne,
　　To fill the vengeful cup.

Aye, every breath they draw,
While bowing to the master's servile rod,
Is fraught with prayer, ascending up to God
　　To plead his righteous law.

One of the best. Composed 1852.

A Brighter Day is Dawning.

A brighter day is dawning,
    And soon it will appear,
When freedom's hosts will rally,
    Then be of good cheer.

I hear the notes of warning,
    They echo through the land,
From Maine's ice-girted harbors
    To Georgia's burning sand.

The people are awaking
    From their lethargic sleep;
They hear the sighing bondman,
    Their brothers groan and weep.

For freedom hath her altars,
    And on them burning fires,
The spirits of our fathers,
    Our noble, daring sires.

And hands and hearts are willing
    To battle for the right,
To break the galling fetters,
    And bless our land with light.

Haste. haste thy glorious beaming,
    My country's rising star,
Millions behold thy gleaming,
    Come, lead the hosts to war.

Marshal thy army, Freedom;
　The contest may be long,
But right must triumph over might,
　And loose the palsied tongue

Then on to victory,
　The battle has begun,
'Tis liberty or slavery,
　We'll fight till we have won.

A mighty work's before us,
　A valiant work to do;
Then let us not prove traitors,
　But freemen bold and true.

Let no one shrink from duty,
　But grapple with the foe;
The wailings of the victims
　Are full of pain and woe.

Ye mountain fires, grow brighter,
　Intenser, till the day
When routed is the monster,
　And vanquished far away.

Ah! longer, burn forever,
　As long as time endure,
When all the living slumber,
　Then burn ye bright and pure.

Old Winter is Here.

O, bright was the spring-time, when gladness and mirth,
   Awoke from their slumbers to hail the green year;
When beauty came forth, to mantle the earth
   In bloom,— but 'tis past,— old Winter is here.

Yes, all the sweet flowers, of Summer have gone.
   And the music we loved now no longer we hear;
The minstrels of nature, Oh! they too have flown,
   Nor lingered to welcome old Winter, so drear.

And Autumn, it came with its glittering sheen
   And painted the woodlands all yellow and sere;
Their beauty and glory no longer are seen,
   They're faded and gone, old Winter is here.

The snow-mantled earth is cheerless and cold,
   Old Boreas is raving,—the prospect, how drear!
The storm-clouds are out, as often of old,
   And all things around us say Winter is here.

He comes o'er the mountain, he comes o'er the lake,
   On hill tops, in valleys, his footsteps appear;
The poor and the needy a wailing will make,
   For Winter, stern Winter, old Winter, is here.

Published, G. M. F., Jan. 23, 1851.

O, Thou Almighty King.

O, thou Almighty King,
Help me thy name to sing,
Thy holiness to bless,
For this, thy righteousness.

Thou dost in Heaven proclaim,
Almighty is thy name,
On earth thou dost impart
This feeling to the heart.

Before thee princes bow
And humbly pay the vow;
All things do to thee bend,
To thee their praises tend.

Thou rulest in heaven and earth,
All things thou gavest birth:
Earth, air, and sea and main,
Respond and shout again.

A thousand orbs that shine
The starry heaven's line;
The moon, the queen of night,
That blesses us with light.

The great and brilliant sun,
That bright and mighty one,
The light of every world,
Thou into chaos hurled.

Around which all things move,
Thy power and wisdom prove.—
Hosannahs sweet and loud,—
He set the rainbow in the cloud!

Hope.

Of thee I sing, how bright a thing,
Clothed with thy own appareling;
It chases gloom beyond the tomb,
While on earth we're traveling.

Oh! while our bark is tempest driv'n,
It points to us the way to Heav'n,
It lights the way 'mong rocks and shoals,
Where billow after billow rolls.

Shedding its light upon the road,
Is pointing heavenward, and to God.

Gems.

Gems there are of heavenly birth,—
Glittering 'mong the dross of earth,—
Gems of almost priceless worth,—
Dazzling bright, of richest hue,—
Beneath the vast etherial blue, —
And loving hearts forever true, —
Blessing the Gentile and the Jew!

Pity.

Pity,—O,"'tis a melting word,
    Then to it be thou given;
And remember that it stirred
    Thy bosom friend in heaven.

Know thou that He came down to earth,
    To save rebellious man?
Within the manger was His birth,
    Who wrought redemption's plan.

O, melting pity, thou could'st move
    Upon the sorrows deep,
Of Him whose soul was only love,
    And cause that soul to weep.

'Twas pity made Him feel our woes,
    'Twas pity made Him love
His greatest, deadliest, earthly foes,—
    The Savior from above.

If pity. then, could make Him feel,
    Who never felt in vain,
Should we, poor mortals, weak and frail,
    Pity refuse again?

O, pity him who pity needs,
    And bind his broken heart;
Pity the thousand hearts that bleed,
    And act the Savior's part.

The world is full of wretchedness,
   Of grief and sorrow too;
Let pity move for deep distress,
   And human pity flow.

Pity the wanderer, him whose days,
   Are full of wretchedness;
For him hope never lent her rays,
   Or shone on Calvary.

His lot was cast, perchance, where vice
   Was taught him from his youth,
Where Satan, clothed in dark disguise,
   Kept back the sacred truth.

Or else in dark temptation's hour,
   He gave away to sin;
One word might saved him from its power,
   And kept him pure within.

We, too, are poor, and weak, and frail,
   And pity need from man,
Let charity on us prevail,
   To pity all we can.

We All are Frail.

We all are frail, each, one and all,
Who dwell on this terrestrial ball;
Each have their faults, their wretchedness,
All stand in need of charities.

Man! dost thou see thy brother err,
   And does he do thee giant wrong?
Let charity, the conquerer,
   With meekness bind thee true and strong.

More blessed far than to receive,—
   Forgive, 'tis noble, good and just;
Forgiving, let us learn to live,—
   Bury our wrongs all in the dust.

For we, too, blindly tread our way,
   And deviatingly we go;
While fancy's flash and reason's ray
   Lend but a transient, meteor glow.

The world is wide enough, and good,—
   Then let us give our fellows due;
A universal brotherhood,
   Will kindly help each other through.

Were we not born for purposes,
   Exalted, holy and most high?
Then let us all our faults confess,
   And live as we would wish to die!

If thou hast genius, boast it not,
　　But strive to make it brighter shine;
Yet all its glories cannot blot.
　　The weaknesses which still are thine.
If thou hast goodness, keep it still,
　　With kindness let thy heart o'erflow;
Have sympathy for human ill,—
　　O, drop a tear for human woe.

And hast thou greatness, mind and heart,
　　Both acting in their higher sphere?
If thou would'st nobly act thy part,
　　Let charity her temple rear.

If thou art wrong, confess it now;—
　　If thou art wronged, O, meekly bow;
Have charity for weaknesses,—
　　Blessing thyself, so shalt thou bless.

Gem.

O, lovely is woman,
Of true beauty possessed.
It makes her an angel,
Her presence ever blest.

My Soul is Longing for Its Rest.

My soul is longing for its rest,
    It would no longer stay;
Then let it fly to Jesus' breast,
    Freed from its mortal clay.

Adieu, vain world, with all thy charms,
    I feel thy power no more;
My Savior stands with outstretched arms,
    On Heaven's blissful shore.

Farewell, dear friends, weep not for me,
    We soon shall meet above,
To spend a long eternity
    With those we dearly love.

The victor comes, the victor, death,
    And now I welcome thee,
Come, take my fainting, gasping breath,
    And set my spirit free.

Come, angels, come, bear me away,
    For Nature's ties are riven;
I hear the song, the blissful song,
    Th' immortal song of Heaven.

September, 1846.

Columbia.

Columbia, when first thou sprung
Forth into life, then round thee hung
Dark threat'ning clouds and angry skies;
The nations looked with anxious eyes,
The storm of war went rolling by,
And thou didst gain thy liberty.

Then looked the nations of the earth,
Much wondering at thy mighty birth,
But soon thy starry flag unfurl'd,
With welcome met o'er all the world,
In every land, on every sea,
Hail, all hail, Columbia.

Brighter than morn, than flowers more fair,
Of virtues many, graces rare,
Blooming among the western wilds,
And crown'd with laurel, deck'd with smiles,
Thy snow-white mantle, purity,
Youthful and fair Columbia.

Yet 'neath thy snowy bosom's fold
The serpent Slavery black had coiled;
He saw thy youth, thy beauteous charms,
And rested in thy snowy arms.

At first thou thought to turn him out
Ere he grew up a monster stout;
Year after year went rolling by,
And thou extoll'd Columbia.

Proud, thy free sons were blessing thee,
And gloried that our land was free;
Thy stars and stripes, on every breeze,
Were floating on a thousand seas.

But hark, that sound from Southern plains
Is not of sweet, enchanting strains,
Harsh and discordant, 'tis the cry
Of thy dark sons for liberty;
Of thy dark sons, Columbia,
Whom thou hast doomed to slavery.

With shame we draw the veil aside
Which would thy sin and weakness hide,
'Tis here the monster we behold,
Who in thy youthful bosom coiled,
His poisonous fangs deep in thy breast,
Columbia,—unwelcome guest.

And thy dark sons in bondage mourn,
Whom for the monster thou has borne
Bastards, not sons, their cruel fate
To meet thy scorn, thy loving hate;
They look for succor up to thee,
Yet sigh in vain for liberty.

How canst thou be deceitful thus?
Part of thy sons with bondage curse,
The other part thy blessings share,
While these defiled thy impress bear?
Thy stain is deep, Columbia,
What flood can wash thy sins away?

Repent, repent, ere 'tis too late,
Down on thy knees, thy sins are great;
In all the bitterness of woe
Let thy repentant tears o'erflow,
So may'st thou find the cleansing flood,
Love all thy children and thy God.

March, 1847, E. R. Morse.

The Past.

The past is gone, gone forever,—
    Never to return, no, never,
Its years of youth, and manhood's prime,
Have floated down the stream of time,—
    Gone, gone forever.

The Land of Rest.

Rejoice, there is a land of rest
  For those who weep and mourn,
A balm for every wounded breast
  By sin and sorrow torn.

While here on earth with them oppressed,
  We languish and decay;
But there forever shall be blest
  With life's eternal day.

Though weary pilgrims here below,
  Our sorrows soon will end,
And then to brighter worlds we'll go,
  While angel bands attend.

No more the pains and ills of life
  Shall each be called to bear,
But joy and peace shall drink up strife,
  And reign eternal there.

Centennial Hymn.

My country, to glory and grandeur arise;
In song and in story a world with thee vies;
The hearts of the bravest in homes of the free,
The hands of the truest do homage to thee.

CHORUS.

O, green be forever,
   The hallowed sod,
Where feet of the pilgrims,
   And martyrs have trod.

Sisterhood of States,
   Phalanx mighty and grand,
Glory now awaits; —
   Lead in Freedom's van.

O, prophets and sages,
   O, heroes who bled,
Far back in the ages,
   Ye labored and led.

O, yet are ye living,
   Aye, living alway,
Down the dim centuries,
   Yet lighting the way.

CHORUS.

 O, green be forever,
  The hallowed sod,
 Where feet of the pilgrims,
  And martyrs have trod.

O, our century past, —
 Saluting the new, —
We hail thee in triumph, —
 In passing review.

Our flag, O, dear emblem, —
 No more o'er the slave, —
Is floating in triumph,
 O'er land of the brave.

CHORUS.

 O, green be forever,
  The hallowed sod,
 Where feet of the pilgrims,
  And martyrs have trod.

Blest star, that prophetic,
 On Bethlehem shone,
With radiant beauty, —
 A glory thine own.

Behold a bright beacon,
 The fairest and best,
The light of the nations, —
 Brightest star of the West.

Far from Europea,
   Her children came forth;
To find thee, blest Freedom,
   Thou fairest of earth.

O, here in the wildwood,
   The wilderness shade;
Their pray'r, and their blessing,
   On thy altar was laid.

Auspicious event, —
   Centennial year;
Our Washington's spirit,
   Is hovering near.

O, Chieftain, Patria,
   The bells sweetly chime, —
'Mid booming of cannon,
   In grandeur sublime.

Unrivaled in greatness, —
   Unsullied in fame, —
O, patriot hero, —
   Immortal thy name.

CHORUS.

   O, green be forever,
      The hallowed sod;
   Where feet of the pilgrims,
      And martyrs have trod.

From ocean to ocean,
  From mountain to sea,
A loyal devotion,
  Our country to thee.

O, Savior, Redeemer,
  From shore unto shore,
May Peace, the white angel,
  Dwell now, evermore.

CHORUS.

O, green be forever,
The hallowed sod,
  Where feet of the pilgrims,
  And martyrs have trod.

The grandest effort of my life; the greatest achievement.—E. R. MORSE.

The Present.

The present is present ever,
Always to-day, to-morrow never;—
Improve the moments as they fly,
Before to-morrow thou may'st die,—
And thy probation cease forever.

A gem.

The Dead.

How silently they sleep
   Beneath the coffin lid,
Within their narrow houses, deep —
   The dead! the dead! the dead!

O, calm and undisturbed
   Their long and last repose;
By a cold world how soon forgot,
   How soon by mortal foes!

On hill and plain they lie,
   In valleys sweet and low,
They heed no more the wind's low sigh,
   Nor Winter's drifting snow.

The husband and the wife,
   The father and the son,
The daughter, and the blushing bride
   Beside her cherish'd one.

And little babes at rest,
   Sleep by their mother's side;
And near, a shaft in Earth's cold breast
   Tells when a stranger died.

The toils of life are past,
   Their pilgrimage is o'er;
The storm that rides upon the blast
   Shall waken them no more.

Published in the Green Mountain Freeman, March 27, 1851.

Time Rolls On.

Yes, Time rolls on, nor will he stay,
    Nor tarry with us here;
Like all things else which pass away,
    So will this fleeting year.

Like all things else which mortals claim,
    Upon this little earth;
It soon to them will be the same
    As 'twas before their birth.

Its home is vast eternity,
    From which it comes and goes;
While each revolving century,
    Back to its center flows.

Each moment as it swiftly flies,
    Gives life a fleeting breath;
But when God speaks, away it dies,
    Dissolved by icy death.

Ten O'clock is Saying.

Ten o'clock is saying,
   Morning well now is past;
Accent strongly laying
   On number ten at last.

Sounds I hear are pealing,
   Those sounds, I know them well,
Gently o'er me stealing
   From that old town bell.

Moments swiftly flying,
   Come quick, stay short, and go;
Quickly they are dying,
   Do we their value know?

E'en while I now am writing,
   The moments some past ten,
Sounds my soul delighting,
   Which sweetly echoed then,

Soon will give me warning
   Another hour has flown,
Tell the hour of morning,
   Eleven now its own.

Hark! e'en now 'tis ringing,
   The old clock's well-known sound;
Time is swiftly winging,
   Upon its voyage bound.

Pay the Printer.

Pay the printer, pay him well,
   Let him have no chance to dun;
How his heart with joy would swell,
His many ink marks, who can tell?
   Pay him ere his work's begun.

Take a paper, read the news,
   Pay for't like an honest man;
You can do it, don't refuse,
It may drive away the blues —
   For a printer sometimes can.

Press and paper, type and ink,
   Labor, labor night and day;
Hands to work and minds to think,
These are needful, — shall he sink
   Just because he needs his pay?

Would you have him do for naught,
   Striving with his utmost care,
Bringing sparkling gems of thought,
As he does, and as he ought,
   Into his casket, rich and rare?

Farmer, follow up the plow,
   Mechanic, raise thy toil-worn hand,
Labor on with reeking brow,
All ye toiling millions, too,
   And pay the printers of the land.

Published in the Green Mountain Freeman, January 23, 1851.

Acrostic.

LAURA ANN THOMAS.

Look on ocean, mighty sweeping,
A grandeur's in her rolling waves;
Underneath are millions sleeping,
Reposing in their watery graves.
Afar in Heaven, brightly shining,

A thousand stars their vigil keep;
'Neath their mantle sweetly shining,
Night's nature softly lulls to sleep.

The things of earth, how beautiful,
How grand, how awful and sublime;
O, be you ever dutiful,
M— thus a laurel'd wreath entwine,
And as your names together span,
So here 'tis Thomas, Laura Ann.

Cousin living in Boston.   March, 1842.   E. R. MORSE.

Thanksgiving Day.

Another year has passed away
Since last we saw Thanksgiving Day,
Another year of time has fled
And numbered many with the dead.

And yet we live and onward move,
The object of our Maker's love,
And truly thankful let us be
That He is ours from infancy.

And watches e'en the cradle breath,
And guards us from the shafts of death,
And all along through blooming youth
Points out the way of sacred truth.

Through middle-age lends life and strength,
And when to hoary age at length
We come from youth and healthful bloom,
He smooths our pathway to the tomb.

Another year of blessings gone,
Another year of mercies flown,
And have we felt those mercies ours,
Those blessings sweet'ning all the hours?

Or must we sad reflections cast
As long as memory shall last?

Our hearts should fill with gratitude,
And nothing else this day intrude;
Should overflow with heart-felt praise
To God, the Maker of our days.

We should remember that His love
Doth her white pinions o'er us move,
And while His blessings on us pour,
Gladly would do for us still more.

Another year has passed away
Since last we saw Thanksgiving Day,
Another year of time has fled
And numbered many with the dead.

Our friends have gone and left us here
To shed for them the mournful tear;
Perchance in childhood they have gone,
And in the morn at early dawn

Have left us to bewail and mourn
That from our bosom they are torn;
Or else, in vigorous, youthful bloom,
We laid them in the silent tomb,

And wept that beauty should decay
And pass so soon with life away;
Or else, perchance, our bosom torn
Bleeds for a bosom friend we mourn.

While all the grief sorrow can know
Is gathered in our bitterest woe,
Our brother, sister, parents dear,
Perchance have caused the sorrowing tear

To sadly fall, to slumber not,
Nor sleep until they are forgot;
If they have not, they may before
Another year has closed the door

Which keeps us from the next, and lay
Them down to moulder, to decay;
Or we may go and leave them thus,
To grieve and weep and mourn for us.

Then let us all do as we should,
And strive to do each other good;
Begin at home the work to do,
And let it reach our neighbors, too.

Let it go forth to all abroad,
And thus obey and honor God;
Then short our life, or short our stay,
Shall thankful be when we can say:

Our work is done, our work below,
To our reward we now will go;
Thus happy ever shall we be,
Possessing it eternally.

December, 1844.

'Tis Noon.

'Tis noon,—rays of the mid-day sun
   Are blessing us with light,
Has half his well-known circuit run
   While in his swift-wing'd flight.

The northern winds blow shrill and strong
   And shake the forest round,
As through the sky it sweeps along
   With roaring, dismal sound.

It blows upon the forest trees
   And bears their leaves away;
Ah! yes. the chilly northern breeze
   Devotes them to decay.

I look and see the waving trees
   That clothe the woodland glen,
Who can but see, that looking sees,
   That Autumn there hath been?

How beautiful to look upon
   This grand and varied scene,
Its Summer robe is partly gone,
   Its robe of Summer green.

'Tis work of Nature, not of art,
   'Tis more than man can do;
Of Nature's work it forms a part,
   And much imposing, too.

The Sea of Life.

Life is a rough, tempestuous sea,
Whose waters never rest;
Whose wild waves beat tumultuously
Against each mortal breast;
Billow on raging billow piled,
Rushes to meet the tempest wild.

We're tossed upon the treach'rous deep,
Where dangers thickly lie,
Where rocks and shoals may cause to weep
Ere we have passed them by;
Though prospects fair may greet our eyes,
Before the angry tempest rise.

How frail each weather-beaten bark,
Laden with precious store!
The storm is loud,—the night is dark,—
Far, far away from shore;
But oh, a beacon light I see,
It is for all—for you, for me.

It is a glorious beacon light,
To light us through the gloom;
Oh, it will guide us through the night,
To our eternal home.
Look on that glorious light afar,—
'Tis Bethlehem's unrivaled Star.

Composed in 1846.   E. R. MORSE.

Reverie.

The Moon is rising in the east,
    The Queen of Night she comes;
Gay-decked as for a royal feast,
    In robes of light she comes.

The glow of health is on her cheek,
    And smiles upon her brow;
Say, Moon, what would'st, if thou could'st speak,
    What would'st thou tell me now?

"To break the slumber from my soul,"
    From darkness call up light,
And cause the waves of sorrow roll,
    Away to deepest night.

O, could'st thou point me to the shore,
    Where sin and sorrow cease;
Where pain and anguish are no more,
    Where all is joy and peace.

Then would my soul within me bound
    Nor wait the coming day;
Released from earth could catch the sound,—
    To bliss would soar away.

Sublimely swell love's wond'rous theme,—
    wide the field expand;
'Tis here only a faint star-gleam,—
    A ray upon the sand.

Revised August, 1894.

Welcome to Jennie Lind.

Welcome, O, welcome, kind welcome to thee;
To the home of the brave, and the land of the free.
Welcome! the cannon sends forth its loud boom,
As the keel of the vessel glides o'er the white foam.
All honor and glory, O mother, to thee,
For bearing this flower far over the sea.

Welcome, O, welcome, the bells sweetly chime;
In harmony mingle, in grandeur sublime.
The people are waiting, sweet angel of song,—
O hasten to meet them,— the temples they throng!

Welcome, warm welcome, thrice welcome to thee,
O, Nightingale sweet, to the land of the free.

Revised Aug. 14, 1894. E. R. MORSE.

The Future.

The future's not-yet ever near us,
With unseen things, to grieve or cheer us;
We know not whether with the morrow,
Shall come to us, or joy, or sorrow;
But O,"'tis safe for mortal dust,
In God alone to put its trust.
The past, the present, and the future dwell
With Him who doeth all things well..?

1850.

There Love her golden harp shall take,
    And chant immortal lays;
Shall bid each joyful tongue awake,
    To join the general praise.

Extract.

Acrostic.

SARAH C. HAVENA.

Sarah is the name I speak,
And acrostic here I seek.
Roses bright, unfold a bloom,
And they shed a sweet perfume;
Half unseen, their beauty fades,

Calm, serene, while evening shades

Hold their sway o'er parting day,
And the red light fades away.
Versed in sevens, here I rhyme,
End'll make of homely chime.
No' more to write, I will rejoice
And sign my name, E. R. Morse.

Second Cousin.

Campaign Song.

Rally, rally, freemen, rally,
  From the prairie, broad and free;
From the mountain, hill and valley,
  Let it echo to the sea;
For Grant and Wilson, tried and true,
  Let the nation's verdict be.

  Glory, glory, hallelujah!
  Our chief is marching on.

Spunky Vermont has been beating,
Our friend Brown, and Horace G.
The Buckeye State, and land of Penn,
Have echoed from each hill and glen,
And send us loyal greeting;
'Neath our flag, red, white and blue,
For Grant and Wilson, tried and true,
  Let the nation's verdict be,

  Glory, glory, hallelujah,—
  Grant is marching on.

Published in Rockford Gazette.

After the Storm.

The scene from strife is changed,
   To one sublimely grand;
Its colors beautiful to see,—
   The rainbow, mercy planned.

Its varied hues are seen,
   All blushing in the east;
The sunbeams glow upon the green,—
   A rich and royal feast.

All nature sweetly sings,
   And joyful is the song,
That through the air on happy wings,
   The chorus bears along.

January, 1843.

Life is a Struggle.

Life is a struggle,
   Oh, all the way through;
Always 'tis old,
   And always 'tis new.

From childhood and youth,
   From cradle to grave,
A battle for right,
   Triumph for the brave.

Acrostic.

ANN M. LITTLEFIELD.

A ransom'd host mightily swelling
Nature's vast theme surrounds the throne,
Numerous millions, wondrous telling,

Mingle with melodious tones.

Lo, what music sweetly pealing,
In gorgeous grandeur rolls along;
There sweeps Nature, godlike kneeling,
The harp's angelic, heavenly song;
Lamps of Heaven brightly burning,
Eternal in their courses go,
Fling their light, their bright eyes turning
In grandeur, all with beauteous glow.
Enclosed is there what I began;
Love true beauty, learn your duty,
Do it, and all is well with Ann.

Second Cousin. Milford, Mass., 1842.

The Silent Land.

Where is the silent land?
    I ask, but none reply.
O, where that far-off strand,
    Where mortals no more sigh?

Over the river wide,
    Our friends have crossed before.
Have reached the other side.
    Silent forever more.

And we soon, too, must pass
    The flood, with muffled oar.
Where none return, alas,
    From that far distant shore.

Where is the silent land,
    Where mortal never weeps?
No mind can understand;—
    Silence her vigil keeps.

Where is the silent land?
    In ocean's barren isles?
Where reigneth silence, and,—
    And nature never smiles?

Where is the silent land?
    In finite, spaceless air?
No sound by breezes fanned,
    Us, spirit tidings bear.

Where is the silent land?
In the etherial blue,—
Where reigneth silence, grand,
Beyond our mortal view. ?

May, 1884.

Acrostic.

JERUSHA HILL THOMAS.

Jehovah reigns, the King above;
Eternal reigns the God of Love —
Rules the nations by his power,
Unfolds His beauty in the flower;
Supports us with His mighty hand;
He heals our sorrows, saves our land.
A world most wonderous He has made;

Has all in order set arrayed;
In earth, in sea, in spaceless air,
Life, light eternal, reigneth there.
Let wonder gaze, our bosom swells,

The heart's its home, nature dwells
Here; here dear cousin may you know
Of virtue's prize, its worth below.
May you through life blest peace enjoy
And happy be without alloy.
So here to you a kind adieu.

Second Cousin. October, 1844.

Summer.

The Summer's last day has come;
    Time rolling has brought it here;
Then Autumn, with its busy hum,
    Brings "the yellow leaf and sere."

The days of her youth have fled,
    Her mid-day hours have flown;
She sinks 'mid her kindred dead,
    Her beauty and glory have gone.

Exulting, she spreads her wings
    Over sea and earth and air;
Now Death her shroud o'er her flings,
    O'er Summer, so smiling and fair.

And who her mourners shall be?
    Who lament the gathering pall,
Who pay the tribute that's due,—
    The tribute that's due from all?

No longer we call her our own,
    She was,— no more is ours,
Her home's the eternal throne,
    And hers th' eternal pow'rs.

Departing, her last words are spoken,-
    Have echoed within our ear,-
A sure and solemn token,
    Succeeds the autumnal year.

August 31, 1842.

The Ashtabula Horror.

Oh, toll the bell!   Oh, toll the bell!
In saddest tones of woe;
Ring out their knell!   Ring out their knell!
Ye seething flames below;
And hissing steam, and blinding smoke,
More cruel than the sabre stroke;
No hand can stay the foe.

Oh, down to death!   Oh, down to death!
In awful crash they went;
All in one breath.   All in one breath,
In horrid burial blent,
No note of warning sent.

Oh, God!   Our God!   We cannot see —
It is thy own dark mystery —
Our voice is mute, our eye is dim,
In vain for succor, look to Him.

The good and bad, coward and brave
Here share alike a common grave;
Our heart is faint.   Upon the air
Floats out that wail of deep despair;
In vain their hope, in vain their plea
Appeals, Oh, God!   Oh, God! to Thee,
That awful wail of agony.

Styled the "Ashtabula Horror" in the newspapers at the time of the accident on the railroad near Ashtabula, Ohio, in which seventy-five persons lost their lives from being crushed or mangled, drowned, scalded or burned to death in this great catastrophe.

The Melancholy Smile.

How eloquently speaks,
   The melancholy smile!
It tells the heart's deep loneliness,—
   One gleam of joy the while.

Behold the trembling tear,
   Moist'ning the mourner's eye;
How hard the struggling spirit strives,
   To choke the rising sigh.!

The swelling bosom heaves,
   With inward grief opprest;
The cold world feels no sympathy,
   For that sad, aching breast. !

And yet with radiance oft,
   The features mutely glow;
It is the melancholy smile,
   Softening the spirit's woe.!

But oh! how many there are,
   The sorrowing ones of earth,
Who feel a sadness all its own,
   E'en from the hour of birth.!

Their grieving spirits bow,
   Their tears bedew the sod;
Their sadly melancholy smile,
   Is known alone to God. !

Published in Green Mountain Freeman, 1850. E. R. MORSE.

Winter.

Lo! from the regions of the north
    Old Winter swiftly glides;
He sends his furious whirlwinds forth,
    While on the storm he rides.

He comes o'er mountain, dale and hill,
    His voice is stern and loud;
And to his most despotic will,
    All things have owned and bowed.

He sealeth up the silver lakes,
    The rivers bind in chains,
Till nature from her sleep awakes,
    And smiles o'er her domains.

Yon forest, sad, and lone, behold,
    Where now his footsteps tread;
It seems like one that has grown old,
    Its youth and beauty fled.

All nature's sad,—for in the tomb,
    Her sweetest flowers rest;
Her minstrels, too, are hushed in gloom
    By their unwelcome guest.

Lo! youthful Spring will break his reign,
    And he will hence depart;
With nature then will smile again
    Each joyful human heart.

1850. E. R. MORSE.

The Cuckoo.

The month of June has come,
    The cuckoo's voice is heard,
Its notes are all gladsome,
    The notes of this sweet bird.

To some, perchance, not sweet,
    Yet truly sweet to me,
Though plaintively it greet
    With mournful melody.

I love to hear its tone,
    Its music in the wood;
Congenial with my own,
    Or, in its neighborhood.

With us, short is its stay,
    The music of its song
Seems centered in one lay,
    Nor is that very long.

O, short does it tarry here
    A pilgrim in the land,
A pilgrim once a year,
    To join the pilgrim band.

It chanteth others' woes
    And bears them to the throne;
Its song poetic glows,
    With beauties all its own.

Fair one, I wish my lot
    Were but to roam with thee,
To visit every spot,
    And pour sweet minstrelsy.

Then nature's solitude,
    At dawn of rising day,
With nothing to intrude,
    Would echo with the lay.

All nature's plaintive voice
    Seems blended in thine own,
And yet, it seems thy choice
    Thus mournful to bemoan.

To some, perchance, not sweet,
    Yet dearly sweet to me,
Though plaintively thou greet
    With mournful melody.

June, 1844.

The Maiden's Prayer.

At eve I heard the voice of pray'r
   In accents soft and lowly;
Gently it rose upon the air,
   Like incense sweet and holy.

'Twas in the silent, peaceful grove,
   Where autumn winds were sighing,
Where budding leaves had whispered love,
   But now were dead or dying.

Her outstretched hands were raised on high,
   With her Redeemer pleading;
The teardrop glist'ning in her eye,
   She, poor and frail and needing.

There in the stillness of that hour
   White angels hover'd o'er her,
And while she sought protecting pow'r,
   Sweet consolation bore her.

She pray'd — but not for length of days,
   Nor yet for earthly treasure;
She wished to walk in wisdom's ways,
   For there were life and pleasure.

This was the burden of her pray'r,
   In accents soft and lowly:
Lord, keep me from the tempter's snare,
   My thoughts make pure and holy.

O, guide me in the blessed way,
Thou great Almighty Giver.
Be Thou my strength from day to day,
My hope and joy forever.

Published in the Green Mountain Freeman, 1846.--E. R. MORSE.

Acrostic.

MARY JANE THOMAS.

May you, fair coz, gentle and kind,
And happy now, forever be.
Regarding virtue, you will find
Your path'll be bright o'er life's dark sea.

Jane is a pretty name, be sure,
And soft and mild is her dark eye;
Nature stands deck'd, lovely and pure,
Embosom'd there is her deep sigh.

The names of those we lov'd, how dear,
How sweet, how soft their whispers seem.
O, may mingle each our tear,
Mary, or do I idly dream.
Acrostic to his cousin given,
Say, shall we meet above, in heaven?

Boston, Mass., March, 1842.

Welcome to Summer.

Welcome, Summer, welcome here,
Fairest season of the year;
Welcome, to the forest bow'rs,
Welcome, with thy songs and flow'rs.

Welcome, said departing Spring,
Welcome, breathes each living thing;
Welcome, smiles all Nature free,
Welcome, Summer, dear to me.

Welcome, from thy Southern clime,
Welcome, smiling Summer-time;
Welcome, with thy genial skies,
Welcome, with thy love-lit eyes.

Welcome, with thy breezy mirth,
Walking, o'er the teeming earth;
Welcome, with thy angel voice,
Welcome, season of my choice.

Thou dost come in bright array,
All things are bending to thy sway;
Roses shed their fragrance round;
With bright garlands thou art crowned.

Thou art on a thousand hills,
By the merry sparkling rills;
And the gushing fountains free,
While they welcome give to thee.

And upon the mountain side;
By the rivers in their pride;
In the valleys, bright and green,
All around us thou art seen.

Beautiful thy garments are,
Smiling Summer, bright and fair;
Verdure springs from last year's tomb,
And the earth is full of bloom.

Singing bird, and busy bee,
Welcome, welcome give to thee,
Welcome from the dewy sod,
Rises, Summer, up to God.

Passing with thy bright array,
Fading, fleeting, is thy stay;
Farewell, Summer, dear to me;—
Last farewell,—farewell to thee.

Published in Vermont Christian Messenger, July 2, 1854.

Go West.

Go thou, and find a Western home,
    Go turn the virgin sod;
Where now the deer and red man roam,—
    For centuries have trod.

Go thou, into the forest wild,
    And let the sunlight in;
Where science fair has never smiled,
    Where art has never been.

Go thou, and hew the giant oak,
    And lay the forest low,
Where ne'er before the echoes woke,
    From woodman's ringing blow.

Go plant the tree of liberty,
    Towards the setting sun;
Hope's guiding star, and victory?
    Shall be thy triumphs won.

    Original composed March, 1854. Revised July 31, 1894.—E. R. MORSE.

How Happy is the Heavenly Throng!

How happy is the heavenly throng;
Of whom I'm speaking in my song.
Happy in God's eternal love,
That ransom'd, blood-bought throng above!

Their God, their Maker and their King,—
His love extol, His praises sing,
Extol His power, and sing His praise;
So glorious in all His ways.

Hark! what pealing anthems swell,
The theme of love on which they dwell;
There He sits on sapphire throne,
While all around His glory own.

Through finite depths of spaceless air,
He reigns the King eternal there. !

Then When Coldness Clogs This Clay.

Then when coldness clogs this clay,
And the tired spirit flies away,
When life's current chilly stands,
And when nerveless are these hands:

When this aching, anguish'd heart,
Feels no more the pained dart,
Then my soul, from sorrow free,
Shall blest and happy ever be.

Then shall it soar to the realms above,
Where all is peace, and joy and love,
Join the ransom'd, blood-bought throng,—
Chant above the rapturous song.

Swell on high the wondrous theme,—
And tell how Jesus did redeem;—
There, forever, sing and praise,
Dying love, redeeming grace.

February, 1843.

Turn Now to God.

Turn now to God, ye young and fair,
Spend in his service all your days;
Live lives of humble, grateful pray'r,
And bless your God with heart-felt praise.

Though now in health and beauty's bloom,
Though now beams bright hope's cheering star,
Yet there awaits a gaping tomb,
And sure, beyond, God's righteous bar.

You know not but to-morrow's sun,
May soon, forever be your last;
Your work, perchance, is nearly done,
And soon your lot eternal cast.

Delay not then till future years,
Shall bring their joys, bestow their gifts,
For you may reap in bitter tears,
When Time the veil of mystery lifts.

Ten thousand snares are in your path,
And Satan archly tempts to sin;
O, then beware to shun God's wrath,—
Beware, let not the tempter in.

Give now to Christ thy youthful heart,
There let the blessed Savior reign;
So shall you, guided by his chart,
The port of endless pleasure gain.

Acrostic.

WILLIAM CULLEN WARNER.

Weep! oh, ye minstrels, pour your lays
Into the ear, the heart of man.
Lo! life was sweet to him whose days,
Like sands, too soon, their courses ran.
Indulgent sympathy, let fall
A tear,—a tear of sorrow on his pall.!
Man lives, but who can tell his end?

Cold is his clay, his voice is still;
Untimely seems his fatal end;?
Light, hope and joy, no more shall fill
Life with their beams,—or glory lend;
Enshrouded deep in death's dark gloom,
No more of earth, but of the tomb.!

Well may we mourn the loss of friends,
A thousand mourn, oh, man, for thee;
Remembered long, thy virtues lend
New, nobler charms, since thou art free;
Eternity is now thy home; !
Redeemed, thy soul no more shall roam.?

William Cullen Warner, a physician, of Bristol, Vt., took strychnine by mistake for morphine for some ailment, thus dying by his own hand.

In the Burial Ground.

I come this calm and lovely day,
And to my kindred tribute pay;
I come once more, O, friends so dear,
And shed o'er you the mournful tear.

I come again with weary feet,
In this sad, lone, and calm retreat;
I walk with silent, solemn tread
Among my lov'd, and sleeping dead.

The day is still, serenely bright,
As silent as the silent night;
A quiet reigns, supremely felt,
Within this seeming firmament.

No plaint of bird or humming bee,
Except it comes from some lone tree;
Or else all sounds the fainter grow
In the autumnal fading glow.

The faint, sweet chipper of the bird,
And squirrel's chatter, low is heard
In the old forest's cooling shade,
In all its glory now arrayed.

'Mong balmy pines, in plaintive mood,
I lay me down in solitude
Among the spruces, bright and green,
And maples smiling o'er the scene.

Yet not a leaf or bud is stirr'd
By welcome breeze or wing of bird,
Among the flowers with fragrance sweet,
Where tread my weary, wand'ring feet.

What scenes again before me rise!
I look and gaze with eager eyes,
I read upon the lettered stone
The time a life on earth begun.

The time of death, number of years
They struggled on 'mid smiles and tears;
No more the strife on this frail shore,
Life's battles past, its conflicts o'er.

Departed ones, each, one and all,
I list, I hear your voices call,
Although the lips are mute in death,
Although has fled the mortal breath,
And eyes are closed to scenes of earth,
Yet here I read, I see your worth.

The hand, the heart, lie nerveless, still,
And yet I feel their pulses thrill,
And voices chanting, sacred, sweet,
Come crowding on this calm retreat.

O, father, mother, here I come,
Once more I see you in your home.
Once more beneath paternal roof,
Once more I hear the kind reproof;

Once more the smile, the stern command
To guide me to the heavenly land.

And now my brother, sister, dear,
Close by your side are sleeping here.
A fond remembrance comes to view,
Takes in the old, new things review:
The kind intent, the thought, the deed,
The mind, the heart, could justice plead.

O, while I view the shaft arise,
Up pointing heavenward to the skies,
A word, a line, reveals anew,
Dear ones, the lost, the tried, the true,
The sad farewell, the smile, the tear,
O, how they cluster, linger here.

The marble, cold and pure and white,
Points upward, through the gloom of night,
To a fair world beyond the skies,
Unknown, unseen by mortal eyes;
Sweet voices call us, come away,
Come, pilgrims, to the realms of day.

A Hymn of Praise.

Again I view the morn,
    The night has passed away,
And now with rosy light new-born
    Beams forth the opening day.

Father, to Thee I raise
    My voice in humble prayer;
O, teach my heart that I may praise
    The God of earth and air.

I thank Thee that my sleep
    Prov'd not the sleep of death,
But that Thy power does safely keep
    And gives me mortal breath.

While some who laid them down,
    Their weary limbs to rest,
May wake to see their Master's frown,
    Or dwell among the blest.

Lord, may I spend this day
    In reverential tear;
O, guide me in the blessed way,
    And be Thou ever near.

O, fit me and prepare
    For all Thy righteous will;
That I at last a crown may wear,
    And dwell on Zion's Hill.

Acrostic.

OSCAR E. MORSE.

Onward, still onward, genius marks its way,
Science and steam, their powers great display,
Connecting links, between effect and cause,
And all in unison with Nature's laws,
Rotating pow'r the greatest burden draws.

Earnest in thought, earnest in deed and name!

Mighty achievements crown the truly brave,
O! see majestic cleave the briny wave.
Right royally the mine shall yield its gold.
Steam pow'r its hidden treasures shall unfold.
Excelsior,—the verdict of the world.

June 27, 1894.

Spring Again.

The winter storms are past,
And now the chilly blast
   Is felt no more;
The spring has come again,
The snows upon the plain
   In torrents pour.

The genial sun comes down
On icy hills that crown
   The vales below;
And there his rays are felt,
Glaciers now slowly melt,
   To ocean go.

The earth comes forth from death,
For, feeling balmy breath
   Of spring, she wakes;
She ope's her wondering eyes,
And hails the genial skies,
   And music makes.

Come down, ye hosts above.
She says in tones of love,
   And let us sing;
A time of jubilee,
Proclaim it joyfully
   To our high King.

And thou, bright morning ray,
Join in the pleasing lay
   And swell the song;
While feathered tribes around
Prolong the welcome sound,
   Which floats along.

A time of jubilee,
Then sound it joyfully
   In tones of love;
While earth, and sea, and air,
Breath forth to Him their pray'r,
   Our God above.

1845.

May Day.

What think you for flowers, our little May queen,
Brought home from her rambles, all sweet and serene?
She brought in her bouquet, and prattled her story,
Pretty flowers, pretty flowers, 'twas all I could find;
I looked all around, and could see no other kind,—
Alas! they were relics of last Summer's glory.

Melancholy Thoughts.

O, why should I sink with dejection and gloom,
   And why to these fellings of sorrow give way?
O, why should I wish that I were in the tomb,
   And this body to dust were mouldering away?

O, why thus with coldness life's scenes should I view,
   And turn away from them my pain'd, weary eyes?
O, why should I languish before they are through,
   The days of my sorrow, whose anguish ne'er dies?

O, God, give me grace, and pow'r to sustain
   This feeble, this drooping, this body of mine;
O, grant me salvation while here I remain,
   While a pilgrim on earth, a sojourner, I stay.

Lengthen not out my days of sorrow and grief,
   Unless for Thy glory my life to prolong,
But whether they're many, or whether they're brief,
   O, change my dull story to rapturous song.

From Satan deliver, from sin, guilt and shame,
   This burden of sorrow away from me roll;
Now give me the courage, the blessing to claim,
   Which speaketh my pardon and maketh me whole.

O, grant me Thy grace, and plunge in the flood,
   O, plunge in the fountain of Jesus' shed blood;
Now wash and make clean, from every foul stain,—
   Come, reign, blessed Savior, unrivaled within.!

January, 1843.

Sabbath Morn.

'Tis Sabbath morn, the sun is bright,
    With glory shines around;
He sheds his warm and golden light
    O'er Nature's works profound.

He looks on earth and sea and air,
    He smiles on sparkling streams,
And all o'er the prospect fair,
    With his sweet morning beams.

The leaf is stirred by welcome breeze,
    Shows forth its ruddy face;
A silence 'mong the forest trees,
    The giants of their race.

The dew is in the flow'ret's cup,
    A lovely sparkling gem,
With rosy lips it drinks it up,
    And wears the diadem.

The fields are white with harvest now,
    With heavy burdens bend;
Follows the sickle, where the plow
    Apart the turf did rend.

All Nature's scenes, of beauty rare,
    A rich repast afford;
All these partake of life a share,
    Are all with plenty stor'd.

'Tis Sabbath morn, the day of rest,
  O, haste to pay the vow;
We soothe our fears, we calm our breast,
  To God we only bow.

September, 1842.

Can We Forget the Men of Old.

Can we forget the men of old,
  Who raised the battle-cry;
Who with prophetic eye, foretold,
  Triumph of liberty?

All fearless, strong, and brave they stood,
  Those souls heroic, grand;
They labor'd for their country's good,
  To save a guilty land.!

They saw our glorious flag unfurled,
  Our starry banner wave;
A mockery to a gazing world,—
  O'er master and his slave.

The Joys of Earth.

The joys of earth, what are they
   But fading, fleeting pleasures?
From our grasp they steal away,
   These dying, earthly treasures.

O, if to-day they give us
   Of pleasure, high emotions,
'Tis but that soon they'll leave us,
   And burst our bubble notions.

If these pleasures we enjoy
   For awhile without sorrow,
Yet will something us annoy,
   And make us trouble borrow.

O, form they a downy pillow
   For us our weary head to lay,
While we upon the billow
   Of time so swiftly pass away?

Know ye that they, like flowers,
   Bloom and blossom for awhile,
Like the winds of adverse hours,
   Flood with tears the playful smile.

When we are fann'd by breezes
   Of fortune and of favor,
And all around us pleases,
   'Tis then we easy labor.

But smiles and tears together,
    Laugh and weep and do appear,
While thus life's storms we weather;
    There's naught abiding here.

Naught abiding here of earth,
    Its joys are fleeting pleasures;
But there are some of nobler birth,
    Enduring, lasting treasures.

December, 1842.

Acrostic.

BEAUTY.

Bright garlands of flowers, O Beauty, are thine;
Eyes glowing with light, stars brightly that shine,
And dewdrops that sparkle, and colors that glow,
Unrival for splendor the bright-hued rainbow;
Ten thousand the forms, in which thou dost appear,—
Youth, Beauty and Love, thy bright images wear.

O, Let Me Rest.

O, let me rest my weary feet,
Bruised and torn with thorns I meet;
The way is rough, narrow or wide;
O, let me rest, some fount beside!

O, let me rest these tired hands,
Toil-worn oppress'd with life's demands;
Painful and sore from day to day,
O, while a pilgrim here I stay.

O, let me rest my burdened heart,
So tired and weary of its part;
Yet beating. beating ever on,
Until the fainting breath is gone!

O, let me rest these longing eyes,—
Looking for heaven beneath the skies;
So quick another's faults to see,
While yet my own may greater be.

O, let me rest my aching head,
When time, and sense, and life are fled,
Upon my Savior's loving breast,
O, let me rest, there let me rest.

August 11, 1894.   E. R. MORSE.

www.ingramcontent.com/pod-product-compliance
Lightning Source LLC
Chambersburg PA
CBHW031439160426
43195CB00010BB/789